The Wounded Line

WRITING FROM TRAUMA SERIES

Jehanne Dubrow, Series Editor

The Writing from Trauma Series publishes accessible books that provide new and experienced writers with practical strategies for representing and exploring trauma—both historically rooted traumas as well as personal traumas—in print and nonprint media. Each book includes writing prompts, a series of best practices for writing about trauma, and suggestions for further reading and research. Appropriate for general readers, use in the classroom, and use in professional non-academic settings, these books offer specific guidance for a variety of genres and media.

Jehanne Dubrow

THE WOUNDED LINE

A Guide to Writing Poems of Trauma

UNIVERSITY OF NEW MEXICO PRESS | ALBUQUERQUE

Printed in the United States of America

ISBN 978-0-8263-6864-5 (paper)
ISBN 978-0-8263-6865-2 (ePub)

Library of Congress Control Number: 2025006810

Founded in 1889, the University of New Mexico sits on the traditional homelands of the Pueblo of Sandia. The original peoples of New Mexico—Pueblo, Navajo, and Apache—since time immemorial have deep connections to the land and have made significant contributions to the broader community statewide. We honor the land itself and those who remain stewards of this land throughout the generations and also acknowledge our committed relationship to Indigenous peoples. We gratefully recognize our history.

Cover and interior design by Felicia Cedillos
Composed in Alegreya

Contents

INTRODUCTION

Real Wounds

There are two essential stories from my childhood.

The first came from my mother's mother, my Oma. It was the mid-1930s in Stuttgart. It was Passover. Everyone in the family ate the fish and then sickened with food poisoning. My great-grandfather was violently ill, but the hospital refused to treat him. He was a Jew, after all. And so he died. A few days after his burial, while the family was still sitting shiva on low chairs, their sleeves torn at the seams in mourning, the SS knocked on the front door. Where was my great-grandfather, they wanted to know. My great-grandmother, a redhead renowned for her fury, nodded. "I'll take you to him," she said. She led the men to the cemetery and pointed to a fresh mound of dirt. "There he is. You can have him." Not long after that, my Oma decided it was time to leave Germany. Somehow, she persuaded all her siblings and her mother to go. They couldn't secure visas to the United States, but there were relatives who had lived in Honduras for many generations. They made a new home in San Pedro Sula. My mother, born after the war, was fed a broth of Spanish, German, and Yiddish swirling together in a single bowl.

As for the family members who stayed in Stuttgart—they did not survive.

The second story belonged to my mother. She was nineteen. One night, the handyman of the building where she lived broke into her apartment. He held her at knifepoint. "Tell me a story," he said. "Tell me why I shouldn't kill you." My mother saved herself by doing as he asked. She kept recounting pieces of herself. She offered to cook him a meal. Eventually she escaped, striking the man with a heavy handbag and then *runningrunningrunning* from his furious hands.

My Oma's story taught me that history is violent and intrusive. It pounds on your door. It pushes you across continents. It forces you to learn new languages.

My mother's story taught me that history isn't the sole figure capable of assault. We are often most at risk in the intimate spaces where we should feel safest—the rooms where we sleep, the rooms where we stack our books on tables, the rooms where we boil a pot of water.

I've written about these tales. Over and over, I've written about and around and toward these stories. They are my essence. If you were to reduce me, the way a cup of balsamic vinegar is heated until it thickens into syrup, you would find these two stories are what's left of me after I cool. There is a sweetness to the narrative of women who have survived. Somehow, they survived. But there is an acrid taste as well.

Yes, there were other stories from my childhood. My father's tales were marked by silence, puncture, elision. At most, he gave me reluctant scraps. Something about a relative who served on the Judenrat—one of the Jewish councils that often cooperated with the Nazis—believing compliance could save his life. The man was eventually murdered, of course.

Something about starved in the ghettos. Something about killed in the camps. Something about shot in the forests.

Something, too, about my father's parents, who came to the United States through Cuba. Something about assimilation. Something about the chocolate and apricot jam of a Sacher torte. Something about the tendrilled smell of black coffee.

My father's version of narrative taught me that the shape, the weight of each story, depends on its teller. Stories can be plump and dense as the raisins in a bowl of fruit compote, or they can be little more than the shadow of powdered sugar sifted over the surface of a cake.

And then there were the narratives I experienced firsthand. The daughter of two career Foreign Service Officers, I was born in Italy and grew up in Yugoslavia, Zaire, Poland, Belgium, Austria, and the United States. I had my first passport picture taken while I was still an infant, swaddled and staring up great-eyed at the camera from my crib. By the time I was three, I had already been evacuated from one country. My mother and I were given only three days to leave Zaire on the last US military plane out of the capital, the two of us sitting on boxes of classified documents for the whole flight. I spoke and forgot several languages. I lived in partitioned nations. I lived in dictatorships. I lived in places where genocide was recent history or else imminent.

Long after all these stories came to define me, I was introduced to the challenges of writing trauma. This was in graduate school in a class called "The Ethics of Representation and the Literature of the Holocaust." The course taught me literature that explores trauma can do many things. First, it can—through a thoughtful, attentive handling of form—put the reader *inside* the experience of trauma. But it can also narrate an experience and make arguments about the nature of trauma itself. In Paul Celan's anguished poems, in the essays of Primo Levi, in Art Spiegelman's graphic narrative *Maus*, I found models I could emulate to write about my own family's encounters with trauma: ways of telling a story that mimicked how pain warps narrative, argumentative structures, and formal approaches.

During my time in graduate school, I married a man who was a career military officer. It was the early years of the second Persian Gulf War, and I was terrified of my husband's work. Although he was in the Navy, and therefore less likely to see direct combat, I dreaded the possibility (quite common in those days) that he would be transferred to serve in-country, perhaps in Iraq or later Afghanistan. As a way of handling my fears, I began to study the tradition of war literature. If I could understand Achilles's rage or Odysseus's grief or Aeneas's commitment to duty, I thought, then maybe I could make sense of why my husband had chosen to become part of the machinery of war.

The poems I wrote—and continue to write—about my military marriage came out of studying ancient and contemporary war literature. Just as I did when trying to learn how to represent the Shoah, I needed literary paradigms as I began to find my voice in the discourse of war. I learned from Homer's Penelope, from Ovid, from Stephen Crane, from the muddy trenches of Wilfred Owen and Siegfried Sassoon, from Bruce Weigel, from Yusef Komunyakaa, and from the poets of later, more recent wars.

A decade later, now a professor, I realized that almost all my graduate students seemed to be working on trauma narratives. I'm not sure if this is because young poets feel pressure—either implicitly or explicitly—to write about trauma or if this is simply an indication of our cultural moment, that trauma dominates our current conversations, shaping how we interpret the past, other people and ourselves, the bodies we inhabit.

Whatever the reason for this increased interest, I saw that students struggled to find support in the creative writing workshop for handling what are known as issues of representation. It's not that they needed someone to tell them what is and isn't trauma. No. That's not a professor's job (and it's certainly not the task of this book). Rather, they needed scholarly and literary exemplars. But most creative writing faculty lacked expertise in relevant fields and were often unable to provide students with appropriate resources and tools.

I began to consider how I might offer guidance in this kind of work. So much of my thinking about how to represent trauma has been shaped by the interdisciplinary considerations of Holocaust and Genocide Studies, which blends literary theory, historiography, psychotherapy, and other fields of research. And I wondered how I might bring this training into my pedagogy.

Scholars often frame the Shoah as a "crisis of representation," one that pushes up against the limits of what an artist can and cannot (or, perhaps, should and should not) transform into beauty. This crisis includes the following problems:

- The problem of representing the past
- The distorting effects of pain on representation
- The impact of pain—that is, trauma—on the continuum of the past and the present
- The strain of annihilation/atrocity on pre-Auschwitz (pretraumatic) methods of representation
- The challenge of representing both genocide and the erasure of genocide

These concerns are modeled on those raised by scholar Joshua Hirsch in his book *Afterimage: Film, Trauma, and the Holocaust.* Although Hirsch is speaking about the successes and failures of movies such as *Night and Fog, The Pawnbroker,* and *Schindler's List,* such considerations can be applied to poems that explore the Shoah as well as other forms of trauma.

For instance, any past trauma may feel elusive and resist our attempts to represent it through art. When the pain is no longer ongoing and is now firmly over, the poet must create a bridge between the present and the long ago. A vanished past inevitably places a strain on our current ability to communicate.

But how do we reach back to a time before trauma? This leap requires the poet to develop fluency in a dialect that no longer exists. To recover who a speaker was prior to the pain, the poet must search for a form of utterance that evokes what has been extinguished. The poet is tasked with expressing an extincted self.

Conversely, as Gregory Orr explains in *Poetry As Survival,* "What certain poets of trauma intuit is that their old self cannot survive the suffering it has experienced without succumbing. Thus *necessity* permits and compels imagination to create a new self, a self strong enough or different enough to move *through* and *beyond* the trauma and its aftermath." And, to return to Hirsch's point, all pain can warp or distort memory. Trauma often causes this kind of rupture, dividing the soul into before and after. As Holocaust survivor Rosa Lublin observes in Cynthia Ozick's novella *Rosa,* "Before is a dream. After is a joke. Only during stays." The during of trauma remains, while the link between past and present is severed. Anyone who has experienced such hurt can understand Rosa's assertion, how the new self is divided from the one that existed pretrauma, how that traumatized self becomes postlapsarian.

Even the final two points that Hirsch outlines can be applied to horrors beyond the Shoah. After great trauma, old methods of storytelling and old ways of handling the figurative may no longer seem appropriate. In fact, poetry itself may feel altogether inadequate, even as the poet wants nothing more than to find a language that expresses the dreadful cry—the scream—of the traumatized psyche. And, finally, it's not simply genocide that leads to acts of erasure. Many forms of trauma are challenging to represent in themselves and are often followed by silence or by outright attempts to expunge the evidence of pain.

There are also ethical considerations that the poet faces (or, for that matter, the novelist, the painter, the photographer, the composer) when it comes to transforming trauma into art. Any poet who examines profound pain on the page might want to ask how subject matter should shape form. The poet might consider who "owns" the trauma. Are there only certainly people who can speak about it? And how should a poet describe the wound itself? Are there parts of the trauma that should not or cannot be represented?

Philosopher Theodor Adorno warns against the "absolute reification" and the "self-satisfied contemplation" of the cultural critic attempting to form scholarly judgements after the Shoah; a scholar may too easily forget the horror that shadows every piece of art we make post-1945. Poets should also worry about the dangers of reification and their own self-satisfied contemplation; writing a poem can be a pleasurable and immersive experience. "To write poetry after Auschwitz is barbaric," Adorno cautions. And yet we do continue to write. We enjoy searching for the most affecting image. We thrill as the meter clicks deliciously into place. When we work on a draft of a new poem that engages with trauma, it is easy to disregard that our lines originate in real wounds.

I would suggest that, even when a poet's subject matter is not genocide but rather some other personal or political crisis, these same concerns might still have value as a part of the creative process. Whether a poet is writing about an ongoing war, an encounter with gun violence, or an experience with sexual assault, to name a few examples, the writer is likelier to produce powerful, nuanced art by asking: What are the best formal strategies to use in recounting this narrative? What research is necessary? What has been written about this subject before? And what is the poet's role in representing this event?

Many years ago, when I was a PhD student, I held a research fellowship at the United States Holocaust Memorial Museum. At the end of my stay in Washington, DC, I was required to give a presentation to the other scholars and fellows. I wondered how I could explain the process of writing poems that represent the Shoah to a roomful of historians, sociologists, philosophers, psychologists, and theologians. My work was so different from theirs. We all handled texts. We all spent hours researching in the stacks. But beyond that? I wasn't sure if I knew how to communicate what poets do.

As part of my presentation, I introduced my colleagues to a list of characteristics that we might look for in a well-crafted and ethical poem that addresses genocide:

- The poem enacts the urgent, formal relationship between the story and the storytelling.
- The poem exhibits knowledge of so-called canonical texts within its field.
- The poem consciously uses and often reinterprets the tropes that populate this literature.
- The poem engages in intertextuality, interdisciplinarity, or hybridity.
- The poem demonstrates self-reflective thinking about its own processes, its position in relation to the trauma, and the ethical challenges of representing atrocity.

I keep this list in mind whenever I write a poem of trauma. I look for these strategies when I read verse that engages with pain, and the poems included in this book reflect these best practices as well.

One of the greatest difficulties poets encounter when first attempting to write about trauma is the certainty that the pathos of the subject matter alone is enough to create a powerful work of art. They may believe that a personal connection to the topic guarantees they will write authentic, moving poems. As a result, people often rely on the horror of the narrative to do the intellectual and emotional work of the text. This can lead to poetry that, at best, engages in cliché, repeating what other poems have already said more compellingly, or, at worse, becomes kitsch. Or, as the great Polish poet Czesław Miłosz says in an essay: "The reality of the war years is a great subject, but a great subject is not enough and it even makes inadequacies in workmanship all the more visible."

Therefore, when writing poems of trauma, it's wise to study the voices that have come before you. Read primary sources. Read theory and scholarship. You can do this no matter the trauma, whether you're attempting to explore an intimate, bodily grief such as sexual assault or you're writing about a large-scale, ancestral trauma like the US government's forced relocations of Native Americans.

In other words, we must do our homework. If we wish to avoid platitudes and triteness, we must understand where our poems fit in the conversation.

For more than twenty years, I have lectured, written, read, and thought about how poets and writers represent atrocity. I've always believed that the examples offered by Holocaust and genocide studies as well as war studies—fields that are interdisciplinary and intertextual—might be useful to poets writing about other forms of trauma. These include historically rooted traumas such as military conflict, enslavement, gender violence, occupation, colonization, and forced migration as well as smaller-scale, more private traumas: the deaths, losses, and abuses that so many poets consider in their work.

There are other disciplines and literary traditions through which we can learn to write effectively about trauma. My scholarly models don't have to be yours. Moreover, the strategies explored in this book are not intended to be prescriptive. These are the techniques I have found particularly useful in my own writing of trauma. Perhaps you will discover additional methods of representation that serve your poems.

The texts I have selected for analysis reflect my training, but they are only meant as a starting point. I believe that each of us should research the literatures and conversations of the specific trauma we hope to represent, whether that pain is historically rooted or is connected to medicine, geography and climate, gender and sexuality, or some other subject matter. We can build a personal canon of texts that inspire us aesthetically and ethically. We can read across genre and discipline. We can ask ourselves the difficult, discomfiting questions.

And, finally, about trauma itself.

The word has its roots in physical experience. Trauma was initially understood as a real wound located on a real body. It was only at the end of the 1800s that the word's meaning enlarged and became as much an agony of the spirit as of the physical self. The fifth edition of the American Psychiatric Association's *Diagnostic and Statistical Manual of Mental Disorders* explains that trauma goes beyond ordinary stresses and losses and is the result of "actual or threatened death, serious injury, or sexual violence." The *DSM-5*, as it's known, doesn't classify stressful events—such as terminal illness—as trauma. That said, *The Wounded Line* includes poems that explore topics like cancer and recurrent pregnancy loss. I'm not advocating for what's known as concept creep, which is defined as "the progressive expansion of concepts of harm." Nonetheless, I believe it's important to acknowledge that, for many readers, these kinds of shattering events may feel like traumas, regardless of therapeutic diagnosis.

Trauma studies blends the work of clinicians, historians, literary critics, and sociologists in an attempt to offer both a theory of and treatment for trauma. Much of literary trauma studies is grounded in Freudian theory as well as in the early work of Holocaust and genocide studies. This includes scholarship by Dominick LaCapra, Dori Laub, Shoshana Felman, Geoffrey Hartman, and Cathy Caruth, who explains in her landmark book, *Unclaimed Experience: Trauma, Narrative, and History*, that "trauma is more than a pathology, or the simple illness of a wounded psyche: it is always the story of a wound that cries out, that addresses us in an attempt to tell us of a reality or truth that is not otherwise available." Caruth understands trauma as a delayed phenomenon that expresses itself belatedly and, as a result, strains the limits of representation. She argues that we must view trauma both in terms of "what is known" as well as "what remains unknown in our very actions and our language."

More recent approaches in literary trauma theory suggest alternatives to this classic model. In an overview of the history of the field, Michelle Balaev explains that contemporary methodologies "acknowledge both the neurobiological and social contexts of the experience, response, and narratives, as well as the possibilities that language can convey the variable meanings of trauma."

Many of the techniques I recommend in *The Wounded Line* come out of the classic model of literary trauma theory; these methods lead to verse that conveys both the known and what Caruth calls "the not-knowing at the heart of catastrophic experience." Other chapters offer strategies that allow for trauma as a knowable, representable experience.

Why blend approaches? Because poets are magpies. In writing this book, I wanted to collect as many formal, narrative, and rhetorical models as possible. When I'm stuck in the middle of a draft and am trying to find the next word, the next line, my concern is seldom with theory (unless theory itself is the poem's subject). Instead I'm focused on practical and immediate challenges: *Do I need a metaphor here? Which part of this story matters the most? What is my argument?*

Throughout this book I contend that in writing poems of trauma we should never forget the word's etymology. Our poetry must find a way back to the tangible and physical. Our language should be informed by the senses, senses that may be heightened by trauma, senses muffled or dampened by pain. Whatever trauma has done to the link between mind and body, that connection—or severance—should be obvious in the poem.

Clinical psychologist Peter Levine writes in *In an Unspoken Voice: How the Body Releases Trauma and Restores Goodness* about the experience of being hit by a car. As he is being rushed to the hospital in the screeching panic of the ambulance, Levine begins listening to the urgent messages that his body is sending to his mind. "I consciously direct myself to go inward," he explains. "I begin to take stock of my body sensations." Within a few minutes his blood pressures drops. His heart rate slows. "Thank god," he tells the paramedic, "I won't be getting PTSD." It's a remarkable assertion. But by engaging in a series of self-protective responses, Levine succeeds in resetting his nervous system and brings himself back into the immediacy of breathing, the heat of his skin, the air moving through his lungs.

In her novel *Thistlefoot,* GennaRose Nethercott creates a narrative that combines ancestral trauma—the nineteenth- and twentieth-century pogroms of the Russian Empire—with Slavic folklore. Near the end of the book, she writes,

> Children were born and raised among the stories, and their children, and theirs, until the stories were forgotten. The ghosts, forgotten, too. Now, a boy whose great-grandfather ate fistfuls of grass to survive drives his rusted-out Chevy in circles between the high school parking lot and the rotary, just to hear the engine purr. A girl whose grandmother was forced into soldiers' beds—a *comfort,* they called her—stays out at a party until three a.m., plays spin the bottle for hours. These, small celebrations. The joys of forgetting. Of running the gas tank to empty just because you can. Of wearing red lipstick and curling your hair, kissing someone, and then walking away whenever you choose. Generation by generation, we forget. Only the body remembers. The body, and the ghosts. Flickers of flame.

Only the body remembers. It recalls the smell of woodsmoke, the velvet touch of a beloved's skin, a sharp crack like a gunshot in the distance.

Ultimately, whether the trauma is rooted in a large, national history or is grounded in a small, personal story, the act of writing a poem is difficult and demands intellectual rigor. Not long ago I gave a presentation about the practical strategies explored in this book.

From the back of the room, a scholar raised his hand, the gesture sharp and furious. I had angered him. "Doesn't it flatten history to use the same techniques as one might employ in a poem about personal trauma?"

I shrugged. "No matter the scale of the trauma," I explained, "the process of representation remains much the same." The poet is always charged with creating a persuasive, three-dimensional speaker, a real body on the page. And the poem's task is to convince a reader that it is truthful, that it possesses some knowledge or insight, that it sees and hears and tastes and touches and smells the injured world.

Writing from the senses is a way of moving toward the cold, shadowed place of trauma. And perhaps, through a language of the body, through the crafting of wounded lines, we can also restore the speakers in our poems, can heal them—however briefly—of their own echoing pains.

CHAPTER 1

Lists and Catalogs

What story can be found in the list, the catalog, the record, the register, the roll?

Many poems about trauma aren't really *about* the trauma itself. Instead, their primary purpose is to represent the traumatized mind—the fracturing of thought, how the intellect tries to piece the broken world back together. As psychiatrist Judith Herman explains in her book *Trauma and Recovery*:

> Traumatic events call into question basic human relationships. They breach the attachments of family, friendship, love and community. They shatter the construction of the self that is formed and sustained in relation to others. They undermine the belief systems that give meaning to human experience. They violate the victim's faith in a natural or divine order and cast the victim into a state of existential crisis.

Sometimes, in response to trauma, the mind organizes. It tries to keep itself within strict boundaries. It looks for forms of containment. In a list poem—a poem that is structured as a catalog of objects, people, places, things—the act of ordering becomes a way to assert control. In his *A Primer for Poets and Readers of Poetry*, Gregory Orr explains, "Poetry is compelling in a crisis not just because it is concise and immediate, but also because it is superbly designed to handle both aspects of experience: the reality of disorder and the self's need for some kind of order."

And it's true that lists do neaten up the world, our lives numbered or sequestered into bullet points. But they are also documents that resist linearity. When we write a shopping list, we scribble down whatever item first occurs to us. Our minds skid through the aisles of the grocery store, darting first toward the produce and then the frozen foods. Tomatoes. Milk. Dishwasher soap. And that's the contradiction of a list poem. The text arranges difficulty into tidy lines while the form remains nonetheless a collection of disparities.

Elizabeth Rosner's lyric essay "The Alphabet of Inadequate Language" serves as the opening to her memoir, *Survivor Café*. As the title indicates, the piece is an abecedarian, a text arranged in alphabetical order. Rosner's use of the alphabet as an organizing principle suggests that this is a primer, an educational tool. The essay offers a comprehensive vocabulary of twentieth-century atrocities, all while reminding us that language is insufficient. The text reaches and reaches again for terminology, but the reader knows even the most capacious lexicon cannot encompass the trauma:

The Alphabet of Inadequate Language

A is for Auschwitz, where more than a million were gassed and then burned into ash. The word that could speak for everything that follows.

A is for *ARBEIT MACHT FREI*, the words on the gates of Auschwitz. WORK MAKES YOU FREE. Except that the phrase is untranslatable. Like so much else.

A is for Atrocity. **A** is for Armenian Genocide, words that are illegal to say aloud in Turkey.

A is for Atom bomb.

B is for Buchenwald, where my father and my uncle were imprisoned, yet did not die.

B is for Bergen-Belsen, where Anne Frank did die. **B** is for Belzec, where half a million were murdered. **B** is for Babi Yar, the ravine and largest-known mass grave.

B is for Birkenau, the "sister" to Auschwitz.

C is for Concentration Camp. **C** is for Crematoria.

C is for Collaboration. **C** is for Communism. **C** is for Churchill.

C is for Cambodia.

C is for Children. One and a half million murdered children. Also the Hidden Children, and the Child Survivors.

D is for Dictator.

D is for Dachau.

D is for Death Camp.

D is for Death's Head Insignia.

D is for Deutschland.

D is for Denial.

E is for Eichmann. **E** is for Extermination. **E** is for Einsatzgruppen, mobile killing squads. **E** is for Ethnic Cleansing. **E** is for Euphemism.

F is for Final Solution. **F** is for Fuhrer. **F** is for Fatherland. **F** is for Forgetting, which both is and is not the opposite of Remembering.

G is for Gestapo. **G** is for Gas Chamber. **G** is for Goering. **G** is for Germany. **G** is for Ghetto. **G** is for Genocide.

H is for Holocaust.

H is for Hitler.

H is for Himmler.

H is for Hoss.

H is for Homosexual.

H is for Hutu.

H is for Hiroshima.

I is for Identity Card. **I** is for Immigrant. **I** is for Ideology. **I** is for I Don't Know How to Go On like This but I Cannot Stop Because the Words Keep Coming.

J is for Jew. **J** is for Jude. **J** is for Jehovah's Witnesses. **J** is for *JEDEM DAS SEINE*, words on the gate of Buchenwald. TO EACH HIS DUE.

K is for Kristallnacht. **K** is for Khmer Rouge and for Killing Fields. **K** is for Konzentrationslager.

L is for *Lager*. **L** is for Lynching. **L** is for Liquidation. As in, the liquidation of the Warsaw Ghetto and the Lodz Ghetto and the Vilna Ghetto, where my mother and her parents were forced to live before they escaped to a hiding place in the Polish countryside.

M is for Mengele.
M is for Mauthausen.
M is for Maidanek.
M is for Murder, Memory, Massacre, Motherland.

N is for Nuclear Bomb and Neutron Bomb. **N** is for Nagasaki. **N** is for Neighbors, the ones who hid Jews and the ones who denounced Jews or denounced other neighbors for hiding Jews. **N** is for Nuremberg. The place of the trials. The place of a nearly impossible quest for justice. **N** is for Nazi.

O is for Oven. **O** is for Other.

P is for Pogrom. **P** is for Prisoner. **P** is for Parade. **P** is for Ponary, the forest near Vilna, where 100,000 Jews were executed. **P** is for Poland, once home to more than 2 million Jews. **P** is for Perished.

Q is for Quarantine.

Q is for Questions That Have No Answer.

R is for Reich. **R** is for Roma, whose numberless dead have never fully been mourned. **R** is for Rwanda. **R** is for Romania, the birthplace of my father's father and the citizenship that saved my father's life. **R** is for Relocation. **R** is for Refugee. **R** is for Roosevelt.

S is for SS, for Stormtrooper. **S** is for Shoah. **S** is for Sachsenhausen and for Sobibor. **S** is for Stalin and for Synagogue and for Soap. **S** is for Sola, the ash-filled river at the edges of Auschwitz. **S** is for *Sonderkommando*, the special detail of prisoners forced to work in the gas chambers and crematoria. **S** is for *Selektion*. **S** is for *Stolpersteine* and for Secrets. **S** is for Silence.

T is for Treblinka.
T is for Theresienstadt.
T is for Tattoo.
T is for Twins, whom Mengele chose for special experiments.
T is for the Thousand-Year Reich, for Terror, Trauma, Tenacity.
T is for Tutsi.

U is for Uprising. **U** is for Underground. **U** is for *Über Alles*. **U** is for U-boat. **U** is for Undesirable. **U** is for Understatement.

V is for Vichy. **V** is for Victory. **V** is for Victim. **V** is for Vanquished. **V** is for Vietnam, the name of a country. **V** is for Veteran.

W is for Warsaw. **W** is for Wehrmacht. **W** is for War, and War, and War.

X is for X. For everything that cannot be expressed in words, for each and every name of the dead that may have been forgotten. **X** is for Xenophobia, fear of the stranger, the Other.

Y is for Yiddish, the almost-lost language. **Y** is for You, the one reading this alphabet and all the ones yet to be born.

Z is for Zyklon B, the gas used to murder millions of men, women, and children in Auschwitz. Now go back to the beginning. See under: A.

"A is for Auschwitz," Rosner's alphabet begins. But soon we are spiraling on to other devastations; the Armenian genocide, for instance, and later, "C is for Cambodia" and "R is for Rwanda." Through the act of list-making, Rosner conjures these atrocities, drags them from history and into the present tense. It's a gruesome magic spell. In this way, the loose structure of a list makes an argument about the relationship between the Shoah and other cataclysmic events, about how this genocide is not only distinct but also resembles other grotesque crimes that human beings have committed in the modern era. Each genocide has its own specific tropes, images, motifs, and terminology but is also deeply connected to other genocides.

The piece ends with Zyklon B, "the gas used to murder millions of men, women, and children in Auschwitz. Now go back to the beginning," instructs Rosner. "See under: A," she orders. Although we've just moved in a straightforward manner through the alphabet, the text ultimately reveals itself to be circular and nonlinear. We will always loop back to Auschwitz, argues Rosner. Through its form, "The Alphabet of Inadequate Language" asserts that Auschwitz is the alpha and omega of atrocity. The message is that trauma and our efforts to understand such pain will form an inescapable ring. The more we know about the trauma, the less we can comprehend it, much less run away from it.

Although I call "The Alphabet of Inadequate Language" a lyric essay, it could as easily be labeled a prose poem; while the piece isn't broken into lines, it employs other devices that we ascribe to poetry, including musical language and associative leaps.

In *Survivor Café* Rosner explores the transmission of trauma across generations. Many children of Holocaust survivors inherited elements of their parents' trauma. These children—who have come to be known as the second generation—often felt as if the ghettos, the deportations, even the death camps were experiences they knew intimately through the stories their parents told. Their parents' memories became their own (received) recollections.

This phenomenon is what Holocaust scholar Marianne Hirsch has termed "postmemory":

> "Postmemory" describes the relationship that the "generation after" bears to the personal, collective, and cultural trauma of those who came before—to experiences they "remember" only by means of the stories, images, and behaviors among which they grew up. But these experiences were transmitted to them so deeply and affectively as to seem to constitute memories in their own right. Postmemory's connection to the past is thus actually mediated not by recall but by imaginative investment, projection, and creation. To grow up with overwhelming inherited memories, to be dominated by narratives that preceded one's birth or one's consciousness, is to risk having one's own life stories displaced, even evacuated, by our ancestors. It is to be shaped, however indirectly, by traumatic fragments of events that still defy narrative reconstruction and exceed comprehension. These events happened in the past, but their effects continue into the present.

Hirsch's concept of postmemory, which she coined in the early 1990s, anticipates developing science. Epigeneticists are currently studying the theory that trauma may leave its imprint in our genes. There was an experiment in which a mouse was a placed in a box filled with the aroma of cherry blossoms. Then the rodent's paw was zapped with an electric current. Soon the mouse came to connect scent with torture—a Pavlovian response. The babies of that mouse were raised in a different box, without fragrance without shock therapy. When the mouse's grandchildren were exposed to the flower's fragrance, they trembled with terror. Upon dissection, scientists discovered that even the animals' smell receptors had altered so that the mice could more easily detect the terrible odor of blossoms.

It is possible that the effects of trauma and the body's response to it are similarly passed from generation to generation, *l'dor v'dor*, as we say in Hebrew. And while the epigenetic transmission of trauma has not yet been proven conclusively, postmemory can be a helpful idea for poets writing not only about the long-term consequences of the Shoah but also about other forms of intergenerational trauma. What is the traumatic inheritance of someone descended from enslaved people? What trauma is handed down from the refugee displaced by war or climate disaster to the child who grows up in another country, with another language, halfway around the world?

List-making is an ancient way to grapple with such traumas. In Lamentations, for instance, Jerusalem and the Temple have been destroyed, and the poet grieves for an entire city. The book is a litany of suffering. It enumerates how grief alters every part of our bodies, our behaviors, our days. Through this exhausting index, the poet reaches a place where words finally run out and there is nothing left to say.

Of course, not every list poem needs to confront the trauma of a whole people. "Lamentations forever bereft," writes Edward Hirsch near the end of his book-length elegy for his dead son—a relentless record of sadness filled with repetitions of what his child loved and who the young man was. Or in Rebecca Lindenberg's "Catalogue of Ephemera," a speaker mourns the loss of one person. The poem comes from Lindenberg's debut collection, *Love, An Index*, a book that elegizes her partner's death, a renowned poet who disappeared while climbing a volcano in Japan:

Catalogue of Ephemera

You give me flowers resembling Chinese lanterns.

You give me hale, for yellow. You give me vex.

You give me lemons softened in brine and you give me cuttlefish
 ink.
You give me all 463 stairs of Brunelleschi's dome.

You give me seduction and you let me give it back to you.
You give me you.

You give me an apartment full of morning smells—toasted bagel
 and black
coffee and the freckled lilies in the vase on the windowsill.
You give me 24-across.

You give me flowers resembling moths' wings.

You give me the first bird of morning alighting on a wire.
You give me the sidewalk café with plastic furniture and the boys
with their feet on the chairs.
You give me the swoop of homemade kites in the park on Sunday.
You give me afternoon-colored beer with lemons in it.

You give me D. H. Lawrence,
and he gives me pomegranates and sorb-apples.

You give me the loose tooth of California, the broken jaw of New
 York City.
You give me the blue sky of Wyoming, and the blue wind through it.

You give me an ancient city where the language is a secret
everyone is keeping.

You give me a t-shirt that says all you gave me was this t-shirt.
You give me pictures with yourself cut out.
You give me lime blossoms, but not for what they symbolize.

You give me *yes*. You give me *no*.

You give me midnight apples in a car with the windows down.
You give me the flashbulbs of an electrical storm.
You give me thunder and the suddenly green underbellies of clouds.

You give me the careening of trains.
You give me the scent of bruised mint.

You give me the smell of black hair, of blond hair.

You give me Apollo and Daphne, Pan and Syrinx.
You give me Echo.

You give me hyacinths and narcissus. You give me foxgloves
and soft fists of peony.

You give me the filthy carpet of an East Village apartment.
You give me seeming not to notice.

You give me an unfinished argument, begun on the Manhattan-bound F train.

You give me paintings of women with their eyes closed.
You give me grief, and how to grieve.

Some of the gifts listed in the poem read like inside jokes. Others are intimate recollections. In particular, the poem is ordered around bouquets of flowers, the kinds of small presents that a man might bring to his beloved, blossoms that resemble "Chinese lanterns" or "moths' wings." The poem is suffused with the scent of flowers, and these aromas lead to the awakening of other senses, to delicious foods and bright colors, to a tactile world in which the two people discover themselves and one another.

A spouse, a romantic partner, can become a living archive. Over the years that person comes to hold a record of all the essential experiences that make us *us*. Lindenberg's poem is comprised of memories, which are by their nature ephemeral. These memories are themselves crowded with ephemera: gasps of fragrance, peonies that will be wilted by tomorrow, snippets of passing conversation. But people are ephemeral too. "Catalogue of Ephemera" grapples with two anguishes. The first is that the speaker's beloved has died. The second is that his death means the disappearance of a library of shared history as well. While the poem does its best to reinvigorate the ephemeral, the text recognizes its own transience. Its lines extend and recede, delicate as whisps of smoke that vanish in an empty room.

Writing Your Way In

1. Write your own abecedarian of the trauma you wish to explore. Create a comprehensive vocabulary that speaks to the personal and public history of this trauma.
2. Using Marianne Hirsch's concept of postmemory, write a poem that explores intergenerational trauma. How have someone else's memories of past pain become your memories? Or, conversely, how have your direct experiences of trauma transmitted themselves to the next generation?
3. As Rebecca Lindenberg does in "Catalogue of Ephemera," write a list poem in second person. Through specific and concrete details, reveal the identity of the "you" in the poem. Carefully arrange the list to create a loose, nonlinear narrative about the relationship between the speaker and the person being addressed.

CHAPTER 2

Repetitions

Why? Why do we repeat ourselves?

We speak again and again to be heard. We reiterate for emphasis: *This* happened to me, this *happened* to me, this happened to *me*, *THIS HAPPENED TO ME*. We retell our stories to prevent them from disappearing the way fog evaporates in the heat of a day. There is also forgetfulness. The repetition may be accidental, a mind slipping away from itself. Like a character from Greek mythology, our echoes might even be longings we follow sadly through the forest.

Or sometimes we repeat our own thoughts because we cannot make sense of what we are thinking. Perhaps we turn over—within the small room of our thoughts—a memory. We touch the serrated past, as if with our fingertips. The past burns sometimes, and we must handle it carefully. The past is a piece of Venetian glass, its stem whisper thin. The past is brittle. The past has surprising contours; we hold it up to the light and study it from different angles, attempting to understand the places it shifts from rough to smooth.

Poems that engage with trauma often use repetition—restating words, phrases, sounds, even images and actions—to convey the experience of the traumatized mind, a mind that may be stuck in its pain, unable to recover from old wounds. Brian Turner's "Phantom Noise," for instance, treats the Post Traumatic Stress of a combat veteran as if it were tinnitus, a ringing within the self. The language clangs from the page. It positions the reader within the constant buzzing of a traumatized body, a place that is both lyrical and electric with hurt.

Phantom Noise

There is this ringing hum this
bullet-borne language ringing
shell-fall and static this late-night
ringing of threadwork and carpet ringing
hiss and steam this wing-beat
of rotors and tanks broken
bodies ringing in steel humming these
voices of dust these years ringing
rifles in Babylon rifles in Sumer
ringing these children their gravestones
and candy their limbs gone missing their
static-borne television their ringing
this eardrum this rifled symphonic this
ringing of midnight in gunpowder and oil this
brake pad gone useless this muzzle-flash singing this
threading of bullets in muscle and bone this ringing
hum   this ringing hum   this
ringing

Turner uses the repetition of the word "this," as if the speaker were attempting to pin down the exact source of the elusive noise, which irritates and distresses him in the way of a phantom limb. "There is this ringing hum," he says, "this / bullet-borne language ringing / shell-fall and static this late-night ringing." The technique is known as *anaphora*: the repetition of a word or phrase at the start of a clause. Anaphora comes from the Greek verb: "to carry back." As readers, we are carried back to the hurt many times over. Anaphora creates a pulse in the poem, insisting that trauma recurs and is inescapable. The effect of anaphora is rhetorical—it makes an argument about how long pain can last—but is also musical.

Each time the word "this" repeats, Turner's text redefines the nature and source of the ringing. Maybe the sound is found here or maybe here or here, the poem hypothesizes. That sound moves quickly from abstract and disembodied to the very real landscape of war in the twenty-first century, where there are rifles and children, "gunpowder and oil." The sound's origin is trauma. Much like a phantom limb, the ephemeral clamor exists simultaneously as here and absent. Trauma collapses the distance between past and present. Trauma is palpable but also invisible.

Reading "Phantom Noise," it's easy to imagine the whole poem as a response to a physician's questions. "What are you hearing?" the doctor asks. And the patient answers, "There is this ringing hum."

Repetition pushes the poem forward. The text speaks breathlessly. And, although there is no punctuation, a reader can create units of meaning. Here punctuation is also a phantom. We can sense where the commas and periods might go. The line breaks feel as if they interrupt the syntax, evoking a sensation of jaggedness, of speech that has been severed. The poem doesn't just narrate the experience of suffering. It uses the rhythm of repetition to mimic that ringing. As readers, we are put inside the buzzing, humming, the "static-borne" singing.

In her poem "Why I don't write about George Floyd," Toi Derricote takes the work of repetition even further. She employs anaphora but also epistrophe, the repetition of a word or phrase at the end of a clause. Given that the poem is about the murder of George Perry Floyd Jr., a Black man killed by police in Minneapolis on May 25, 2020, Derricote's formal choices make sense. The poem repeats itself to mimic the awful repetition of history, that so many Black men have been murdered by police officers so many times before.

Why I don't write about George Floyd

Because there is too much to say
Because I have nothing to say
Because I don't know what to say
Because everything has been said
Because it hurts too much to say
What can I say what can I say
Something is stuck in my throat
Something is stuck like an apple
Something is stuck like a knife
Something is stuffed like a foot
Something is stuffed like a body

Derricote's poem is about the insufficiency of poetic speech. A poem is not up to the task of confronting George Floyd's murder, the text argues. His death is too big for verse, leaving the speaker without argument, without some new insight to offer. His death is too painful for words.

And yet here is the poet writing the very poem she says she doesn't write. Derricote says of the piece,

> There was so much that my parents and grandparents, escaping from the violence of the South and their own personal histories of trauma, didn't (and wouldn't!) talk about. They didn't want their children to grow up with the same fears. We had to move on. The killing of George Floyd brought up a grief that feels as though it had been put away for centuries. The poem is about the long, hard process of reclamation.

With its title, the poem offers a thesis: I do not write about George Floyd. First, the speaker agrees with this assertion. Because, she argues. Because. Because. Because. Because. The opening five lines offer five different explanations for why the murder is unsayable.

Then comes the line, "What can I say what can I say." It appears at the precise midpoint of the poem. The line function as a hinge. It's a cry of uncertainty that divides the text in two. The line itself can be bisected into "What can I say" and "what can I say." This pair of exclamations runs together. No punctuation slows the speaker's anguish.

If the first half of the poem is a clinical explanation for why Floyd's death defies the craft of poetry, then the second half is a visceral attempt to express the death, how it leaves the poet both incapable of speech and compelled to communicate.

The final five lines are bodily. Now they center on image rather than on idea. Maybe, the poem seems to suggest, the only way to speak about George Floyd is by returning to physical sensation, sense-driven language. "Something is stuck in my throat," the speaker says. Her struggle to express grief echoes the way in which Floyd was murdered, asphyxiated by a policeman who knelt on his neck for nine minutes and twenty-nine seconds.

"Something is stuck like an apple / Something is stuck like a knife," writes Derricote. Now we are in the world of ancient storytelling. The apple and the knife are objects that evoke myth, fairytale, the Bible. They are motifs of sin, sacrifice, or revenge.

"Something is stuffed like a foot / Something is stuffed like a body," the poem ends. Derricote shifts the verb from "stuck" to "stuffed." Her use of alliteration, the pairing of identical sounds at the start of words, is another form of repetition. She moves us from the speaker's passive experience of silence to being actively silenced by someone else. Floyd's murder—that his voice was stopped as he tried to call out, *I can't breathe*—haunts the text. Haunts the speaker. Haunts the reader.

Sometimes we write poetry in response to horror because we can't help ourselves. Even if the act of writing feels unseemly, a poet may need to speak, to find a language for the unspeakable. "Why I don't write about George Floyd" articulates the painful relationship between trauma and the impulse of the artist to represent that pain. Through its grieving, halting repetitions, the poem enacts this struggle. The poem fights with itself. It resists an easy ending.

Writing Your Way In

1. Write about a routine activity from your daily life, something physical that involves a repetitive motion. If you associate this activity with trauma, avoid naming the pain directly. Instead, repeat a noun or a verb to evoke that trauma. Whenever you find yourself stuck in the draft, use that repetition to find new momentum.
2. Using "Phantom Noise" as a guide, describe a psychic pain through the language of a physical injury or ailment. Is the trauma like a sprained ankle? Like shortness of breath or asthma? Like a stomachache? Like a stiff neck?
3. Emulate the structure of "Why I don't write about George Floyd," allowing the body of the poem to be an answer to the poem's title. Incorporate repetition both at the beginnings and endings of lines. Avoid punctuation.

CHAPTER 3

Songs

How do we sing about the dark times?

In the late 1930s, having left Nazi Germany like so many intellectuals of the time, poet and playwright Bertolt Brecht continued his work in Denmark. His *Svendborg Poems*, published in 1939, includes these brief lines, as translated by David Constantine and Tom Kuhn:

> In the dark times
> Will there be singing?
> There will be singing
> Of the dark times.

The poem's opening question implies that we shouldn't sing in an era of shadow. Some things are so awful they must defy music.

But the poem answers its own query. It says: yes, we will sing, and the darkness will become our subject. Maybe the darkness will snuff out everything else. Maybe the darkness is so wide that our only topic must be this current horror.

According to Brecht's verse, a song of trauma is a circular one. It turns on itself. It turns toward itself. It is sharply aware of the circumstances in which it comes to be. It knows its origins. It knows that its melody resembles fog and night. The poem's ending surprises, but it also feels inevitable. What else could we sing in dark times but the dark itself? In authoritarian eras, the alternative to song is silence. And for the artist, Brecht implies, singing out must be the only possible choice. Signing is defiance. It is resistance and survival.

The poem whose subject matter is song doesn't argue that poetry and singing are identical. Instead, this kind of poem often explores the ways in which ordinary speech might be insufficient during dark times. The poem understands the tradition it enters, such as the ancient Psalms, which rejoiced and lamented and grieved. Perhaps it engages with Whitman's *Song of Myself*, the song sequences of e.e. cummings, Berryman's Dream Songs, or the Matins and Vespers in Louise Glück's *The Wild Iris*, to name a few examples. Poems that explore song acknowledge how a melody is often understood regardless of tongue. A tune conveys its meaning, whatever one's nation-state. These poems announce: I am not a song, but I want to understand the euphony of words.

Such poems are frequently attentive to sonorous effects of sound and rhythm, two of the elements that make a poem lyrical. In Soul Vang's "Song of the Cluster Bomblet," the poet speaks through the seductive persona of an explosive weapon. The poet wears a mask. In this case, Vang—a US Army veteran—talks in the voice of an inanimate object whose purpose is to murder and devastate. The cluster bomblet's descriptions are beautiful and sensory. In cutting, brief lines, the little bomb sings a song of itself.

Song of the Cluster Bomblet

I am a seed
Of the tree of knowledge.

I arrived here
In mother's steel womb—

A snug, dark pod—
With my hundred siblings.

On impact, her womb opened
And we scattered hundreds of yards.

I am a blue ridged-winged ball,
Created to appeal

To any child's senses
Of beauty and curiosity.

When a child finds me,
Buried among roots of berries

Or wild flowers,
And cradles me

In her warm hands,
My heart melts.

Vang gives the cluster bomblet human characteristics, a point of view. This technique renders the weapon even more terrifying. Now, the bomb comes from a womb. It's mammalian. It has a heart that responds to the warmth of a child's hands. The more alive and organic the cluster munition becomes, the more it resembles us. And the fact that the bomblet can sing? Well, that's a painful thought too. We want to believe that music and its beauty have a moral component. "Song of the Cluster Bomblet" reminds readers that what is alluring and what is good don't always rhyme.

By speaking in the voice of a cluster bomblet, Vang creates intellectual distance. He could approach the trauma of war directly, from his own experiences as a soldier, but the persona allows him greater opportunity to experiment than a more explicitly autobiographical poem might permit. The poet too was once trained to be a weapon of war. In entering the perspective of an inanimate, murderous object, Vangs uses first-person singular, but it is not the I (or the eye) of autobiography. Instead, he communicates from a place of imagination; he inhabits the body of the bomb. As a result, the poet can take more risks—emotionally, aesthetically, ethically—than if he had spoken from his personal history as a soldier.

Not every poem about song focuses solely on the lyrical, emphasizing the musical qualities of language. Some poems shift their attention toward narrative, toward storytelling in verse. Brigid Pegeen Kelly's "Song" sounds as if could be a fairytale or a strange piece of folklore, a terrible fable about violence and love.

Song

Listen: there was a goat's head hanging by ropes in a tree.
All night it hung there and sang. And those who heard it
Felt a hurt in their hearts and thought they were hearing
The song of a night bird. They sat up in their beds, and then
They lay back down again. In the night wind, the goat's head
Swayed back and forth, and from far off it shone faintly
The way the moonlight shone on the train track miles away
Beside which the goat's headless body lay. Some boys
Had hacked its head off. It was harder work than they had imagined.
The goat cried like a man and struggled hard. But they
Finished the job. They hung the bleeding head by the school
And then ran off into the darkness that seems to hide everything.
The head hung in the tree. The body lay by the tracks.
The head called to the body. The body to the head.
They missed each other. The missing grew large between them,
Until it pulled the heart right out of the body, until
The drawn heart flew toward the head, flew as a bird flies
Back to its cage and the familiar perch from which it trills.
Then the heart sang in the head, softly at first and then louder,
Sang long and low until the morning light came up over
The school and over the tree, and then the singing stopped. . . .
The goat had belonged to a small girl. She named

The goat Broken Thorn Sweet Blackberry, named it after
The night's bush of stars, because the goat's silky hair
Was dark as well water, because it had eyes like wild fruit.
The girl lived near a high railroad track. At night
She heard the trains passing, the sweet sound of the train's horn
Pouring softly over her bed, and each morning she woke
To give the bleating goat his pail of warm milk. She sang
Him songs about girls with ropes and cooks in boats.
She brushed him with a stiff brush. She dreamed daily
That he grew bigger, and he did. She thought her dreaming
Made it so. But one night the girl didn't hear the train's horn,
And the next morning she woke to an empty yard. The goat
Was gone. Everything looked strange. It was as if a storm
Had passed through while she slept, wind and stones, rain
Stripping the branches of fruit. She knew that someone
Had stolen the goat and that he had come to harm. She called
To him. All morning and into the afternoon, she called
And called. She walked and walked. In her chest a bad feeling
Like the feeling of the stones gouging the soft undersides
Of her bare feet. Then somebody found the goat's body
By the high tracks, the flies already filling their soft bottles
At the goat's torn neck. Then somebody found the head
Hanging in a tree by the school. They hurried to take
These things away so that the girl would not see them.
They hurried to raise money to buy the girl another goat.
They hurried to find the boys who had done this, to hear
Them say it was a joke, a joke, it was nothing but a joke. . . .
But listen: here is the point. The boys thought to have
Their fun and be done with it. It was harder work than they
Had imagined, this silly sacrifice, but they finished the job,
Whistling as they washed their large hands in the dark.
What they didn't know was that the goat's head was already
Singing behind them in the tree. What they didn't know
Was that the goat's head would go on singing, just for them,

Long after the ropes were down, and that they would learn to listen,
Pail after pail, stroke after patient stroke. They would
Wake in the night thinking they heard the wind in the trees
Or a night bird, but their hearts beating harder. There
Would be a whistle, a hum, a high murmur, and, at last, a song,
The low song a lost boy sings remembering his mother's call.
Not a cruel song, no, no, not cruel at all. This song
Is sweet. It is sweet. The heart dies of this sweetness.

Although "Song" isn't broken into rhyming quatrains, in many ways it functions as a traditional ballad might: it is verse that tells a dramatic story, its lesson is ancient (as if the text has been transmitted across many generations), and its power lies in the force of its striking images. Like many traditional ballads, "Song" is about violence and retribution.

Ballad comes from the Old French word for "dancing song," *ballade*; these were poems meant to be sung for an appreciative audience, perhaps villagers gathering in a great hall, eager for the night's long entertainment. "Listen," Pegeen Kelly's speaker begins. And, later, she urges again, "But listen." The poem asks us to engage with the tale of the girl and the goat and the boys. We don't merely read the text. We participate in its music, avid spectators to the hard work of killing. Broken Thorn Sweet Blackberry's song becomes our melody, and, when the animal is murdered, we feel the girl's loss as if it were our own. When the goat's head sings in the tree, we too are plagued—as the boys are—by this death that can't be undone, the song of the dead creature not "cruel" but "sweet," devastating in its sweetness.

I had a teacher who used to say, "A poem must have both roots and wings." The narrative elements ground the poem. They root the text in the solidity of things. The lyric qualities give the poem flight, allowing it to soar up and through us. Brigid Pegeen Kelly's remarkable "Song" certainly possesses both roots and wings. It's a modern-day ballad that balances the narrative and the lyric. We are pulled into the story and then propelled upward by its singing—"it was a joke, a joke, it was nothing but a joke."

The poem that explores song often argues that grief is a kind of melody. Trauma has its own music. Our task is to find the tune.

Writing Your Way In

1. Write a poem that, like Brecht's, asks and then answers its own question. Include some element of song or singing in the draft.
2. As with "Song of the Cluster Bomblet," write a poem in the voice of an inanimate object that represents some facet of your trauma (e.g. "Song of Rohypnol," "Song of the Checkpoint"). What music does this object produce? Focus on the lyrical qualities of your language. Use the distance created by the persona to surprise yourself.
3. Write a folk story or fairytale whose subject is trauma. Include both human and animal characters. Emulate Brigid Pegeen Kelly's "Song," attempting to find a balance between narrative and lyric. Allow something or someone to sing in the poem.

CHAPTER 4

Fugue States

What is the sound of trauma? How do we escape the pain?
How do we run toward it?

Beyond a general consideration of song, poems that represent trauma frequently engage with a very specific musical form: that of the fugue. In a fugue, a theme is introduced and is then repeated or imitated. The lines of music move contrapuntally, interweaving and overlapping. The fugue is a chance for the composer to show off skill and dexterity, to demonstrate how the harmonies dovetail just as one piece of wood might slot perfectly into another, no space for error, only the clean cuts of craftsmanship. Think Johann Sebastian Bach. Think Mozart or Brahms. Once a fugue starts, the music can feel as if it has neither beginning nor end. It becomes a constant spiral of sound, dizzy and hypnotic.

And here's the pleasure of language: a fugue can also be a psychological state in which an individual experiences dissociation and displacement, usually as a response to extreme trauma. Poems that gesture toward a fugue generally try to evoke both meanings of the word. In their explorations of trauma, these poems incorporate repetition, motifs and themes that overlap like chains of notes strung together, as well as disorienting images and metaphors.

Paul Celan—a German-speaking Romanian Jew who was imprisoned in a labor camp during World War II—wrote arguably the most famous and influential poem in Holocaust literature. His "Todesfuge" (translated by John Felstiner as "Deathfugue") enacts the dual meanings of the word; the text functions both as an artifact of testimony and as a rigorous example of poetic craft. The poem has cast a long shadow, not only defining a poetics of the Shoah but also helping to establish the obsessive, recursive music of trauma literature.

On the internet, there are recordings of Paul Celan reading from "Todesfuge." Even someone who does not understand German can hear the trancelike momentum of the poem; as in a musical fugue, it lurches forward through themes and variations. The poem occupies the uncanny landscape that the French intellectual and Holocaust survivor David Rousset once called the concentrationary universe, *l'univers concentrationaire*.

In "Todesfuge," Celan guides the reader through a death camp, speaking in first-person plural, a collective voice of pain. We slide back and forth between the squalor and filth of life for the Jewish prisoners—embodied by the Biblical figure Shulamith, the Shulamite woman who appears in the *Song of Songs*—and the blonde, glittering power of the Nazis—embodied by Margarete, the love interest in Goethe's *Faust*. Celan positions Shulamith as a counterpoint to Margarete. If the former represents the historical suffering and trauma of the Jews, then Margarete signifies the shining, enticing beauty of German culture. Shulamith is a figure of smoke and ash, while Margarete is golden-haired. Through its handling of refrains—its chorus-like repetitions of lines and phrases—"Todesfuge" pushes forward, like a train rumbling across the tracks, even as the mind of the poem whirls in a dissociative fugue, unable to escape the hallucinatory landscape of the Shoah.

Valerie Bandura's "Breathing Ground" follows in the tradition of Celan. Her fugue-like poem considers what is often referred to as the "Holocaust by bullets." In the early 1940s, Nazi mobile killing units coopted local citizens across Ukraine to assist in the murder and mass burial of approximately 1.5 million of their Jewish neighbors. These exterminations occurred not in the infamous gas chambers of

Treblinka or Chełmno but at close range, often with a gunshot to each head. The murders took place in forests, at the edges of small villages, near ravines. Then the earth was shoveled over.

"Breathing Ground" is a breathless, relentlessly musical piece that opens with a layering of rhyme, matching sounds to mimic the noises of those buried alive. Not everyone who was shot died immediately in the mass graves. The ground often moved with life for many days after.

Breathing Ground

To tell a long story short

it went on for days   like this

up and down up and down   the ground

groaned as it rose   domed into a mound

of human   and dirt body   of earth as a muscle

grew and moaned from a wound

under a thin layer of hoof-stamped

ground   not still not sound

not here there   not now then   when

they were done   they were not done

with the dead were   not even dead

in the ground   the dead were breathing

ground in the ground   rising as one

lung as one   body as one   godawful song

lifting the ground from the ground   groaning

from the strain in my diaphragm now   in the car

on the couch   in the middle of the grocery store

lost in the parking lot   curled on the floor

first a gasp then   a heave then   the downpour

of bodies strewn like clothes   my clothes here   33°26'21.9"N 111°37'24.8"W

and there   48°41'03.0"N 26°27'31.7"E

and there   48°57'00.0"N 26°34'37.4"E

and there   48°40'23.1"N 26°34'30.9"E

and there   48°40'57.1"N 26°33'33.7"E

and there   48°41'40.5"N 26°33'35.0"E

and there   49°35'41.9"N 27°27'53.4"E

and there   50°27'23.5"N 26°54'14.4"E

and there   49°36'00.5"N 27°37'00.8"E

and there   49°58'00.1"N 27°13'00.1"E

and there 50°24'00.0"N 27°10'59.9"E

and there 49°36'47.0"N 26°31'20.7"E

and there 49°30'00.0"N 26°45'00.0"E

and there 50°06'56.8"N 26°49'23.8"E

and there 50°07'53.1"N 27°29'40.9"E

and there 50°11'00.6"N 27°03'53.4"E

and there 50°17'34.3"N 26°51'21.9"E

and there 48°45'00.0"N 27°04'00.1"E

As the speaker contemplates the killing of her ancestors, she is gradually dragged into the horrifying fugue of the past, so that she feels herself to be *almost* among the dead and dying. Even when she remains sitting "in the car" or "on the couch," the trauma of the Shoah gasps inside her, visceral and ineluctable. Then, halfway through, the text suddenly cycles into an awful, new refrain. All narrative is abandoned, and the poem begins to recite a sequence of coordinates on a map. For the remainder of the piece, the speaker moves between her present-day location in Arizona and different sites of horror in Ukraine. All physical sensation disappears. The frightening, bodily music that opened the poem is replaced by the wintry tune of numbers, each coordinate different but also difficult to distinguish from the others, the numbing repetition of "and there."

Beyond representations of historically rooted traumas such as genocide, the fugue is also well-suited to exploring quieter, more private traumas. Suji Kwock Kim has said of her poem "Fugue" that its title "derives from the Latin, *fuga*, etymologically related to both *fugare* ('to chase') and *fugere* ('to flee'). The poem went through several drafts, as I was going through several miscarriages. It's dedicated to my son."

Kim's "Fugue" is a poem about how bodily trauma can lead to psychic trauma, those intimate losses of each fetus devastating, a grief that the mind both lurches toward and attempts to escape. The rhythm of the poem isn't fugue-like in the way of Celan's "Todesfuge" or Bandura's "Breathing Ground." Rather, it's the long accumulation of clauses within complex sentences that begins to cast a spell on the reader, putting us inside the experience of loss.

Fugue

Out of albumen and blood, out of amniotic brine,
placental sea-swell, trough, salt-spume and foam,

you came to us infinitely far, little traveler, from the other world—
skull-keel and heel-hull socketed to pelvic cradle,

rib-rigging, bowsprit-spine, driftwood-bone,
the ship of you scudding wave after wave of what-might-never-have
    been.

Memory, stay faithful to this moment, which will never return:
may I never forget when we first saw you, there on the other side,

still fish-gilled, water-lunged,
your eelgrass-hair and seahorse-skeleton floating in the sonogram
    screen

like a ghost from tomorrow,
moth-breath quicksilver in snowy pixels, fists in sleep-twitch,

not yet alive but not *not*,
you who were and were not,

a thunder of bloodbeats sutured in green jags on the ultrasound
machine
like hooves galloping from eternity to time,

feet kicking bone-creel and womb-wall,
while we waited, never to waken in that world again,

the world without the shadow of your death,
with no you or not-you, no *is* or *was* or *might-have-been* or *never-were*.

May I never forget when we first saw you in your afterlife
which was life,

soaked otter-pelt and swan-down crowning,
face cauled in blood and mucus-mud, eyes soldered shut,

wet birth-cord rooting you from one world to the next,
you who might not have lived, might never have been born, like all
the others,

as we looked at every pock and crook of your skull,
every clotted hair, seal-slick on your blue-black scalp,

every lash, every nail, every pore, every breath,
with so much wonder that wonder is not the word—

Note the poet's use of those compound words: otter-pelt, swan-down, mucus-mud, birth-cord, seal-slick, blue-black. Nouns and verbs are tethered together by hyphens like umbilical cords. The images are elemental, creaturely. It's as if the trauma of miscarriage demands a new language of the speaker. In *The Body in Pain: The Making and Unmaking of the World*, scholar Elaine Scarry writes,

> Whatever pain achieves, it achieves in part through its unsharability, and it ensures this unsharability through its resistance to language. . . . Physical pain does not simply resist language but actively destroys it, bringing about an immediate reversion to a state anterior to language, to the sounds and cries a human being makes before language is learned.

At times, trauma and its immersive effects strain the limits of speech. In such cases, we must invent a new vocabulary if we wish to express how it too is unsayable and unsharable.

Writing Your Way In

1. Write a poem that includes at least two fugue-like refrains (hint: it's best to pick lines or phrases that are compelling). Allow the repetitions to create a push-pull in the draft, a tension between the immersive qualities of a musical fugue and the impulse to flee, which is a symptom of a dissociative fugue.
2. Write a poem that experiments with the fugue's duality as a thing that both chases and flees. How is the speaker pursued by trauma? How does the speaker chase after that hurt?
3. Write a poem that invents new language to speak about trauma. Use compound words. Turn nouns into verbs. Explore how pain can stretch the boundaries of language.

CHAPTER 5

Obliquities

What if we cannot approach the trauma? What if we must look at it sideways, around a sharp corner?

Trauma can resemble a solar eclipse: dangerous to look at directly. Such head-on viewings can cause permanent damage. There are traumas that can only be confronted through pinhole projections. Or, if we glance at them, our contact must be quick, like fingertips touching the handles of a pot: brief and uncertain, to determine how much heat the metal still holds.

As with the fugue state, an oblique approach to representing trauma—one in which the speaker explores pain circuitously—allows the reader to enter the sensation of trauma. It's a form of mimicry. The poem imitates how the traumatized mind may avoid direct confrontations with its hurt. This evasiveness often permeates the poem's voice, its choice of images, and its argument.

Take, for instance, Beth Bachmann's "Mask." The poem captures the collective trauma of the COVID-19 pandemic, which, in the spring of 2020, forced many millions of people around the world into quarantine, social distancing, and other measures to stay safe. In evasive and elliptical couplets, the speaker narrates the strangeness of that terrifying time.

Mask

During our self-isolation, you send me collages
of God's blown animals, breathed into, heated

and shaped like glass. Our skin is full of holes
for oil and sweat. When I whisper, *Breathe me in*,

I mean all of me—the scent of my flesh, but also me,
my god, the beginning of the fulfillment of this desire.

In a mask, you can be whoever I want you to be, king
or dog: *muse* comes from *muzzle*, to track your kill.

The plague doctors wore masks in the shape of a bird,
the beak filled with fresh clippings: juniper, rose, clove.

The mask is a type of respirator, meaning breathe again,
which is how we've managed to stay alive all these years.

Through the glass eyes, they could examine the body
they could not touch with their bare hands.

Breath can be both instinctive and controlled.
Matisse's most famous cutout is "Blue Nude II,"

a woman who appears to be made of parts, but who
was scissored instead from a single sheet of paper.

Bachmann spends the first half of the poem exploring the tension between a longing for closeness and a fear of intimacy, the permeability of bodies, the danger of contagion. The face mask—ubiquitous during that pandemic era—is a protective measure. But the speaker chooses to see these masks as a source of desire; the cloth, which covers a wearer's nose and mouth, resembles something a lover might put on as a form of kink, a fetish. The mask is dress-up, turning the wearer into "king / or dog."

But then the piece makes an abrupt swerve: "*muse* comes from *muzzle*, to track your kill." Despite her efforts to forget the mask's medical function, the speaker can't ignore the presence of death and disease. Now she remembers the medieval "plague doctors" who "wore masks in the shape of a bird," scented herbs placed inside the hollow beak to hide the stench of the Black Death. Behind their fowl-faced masks, these doctors are able to keep the trauma at a distance, never forced to touch bodies "with their bare hands."

In the final four lines, the poem makes another turn. The speaker considers Matisse's "Blue Nude II," a collage that appears to be made of many separate pieces of paper but is, in fact, comprised of "a single sheet." Matisse's paper cutouts reduce a body to its basic forms. In the way of Matisse's art, the poem seems to be "made of parts," disparate and evasive components that Bachmann has glued together. The poem too has the detachment of a plague doctor viewing the world "through the glass eyes" of a mask. The speaker is cold, dispassionate, as if it might be dangerous to recall the pandemic with too much emotion, as if feeling itself were a contagion.

And let's not ignore the speaker's earlier assertion that "*muse* comes from *muzzle*." The origins of "muzzle" are uncertain, but it's thought that its roots might be found in the Old French word for "snout." Bachmann uses etymology to guide the reader into a landscape where meaning shifts constantly. Both language and our ethics are rendered unstable. Bachmann ties creativity to constraint, muse and muzzle brought together in a single line. Ultimately, "Mask" is a poem that confronts an uncomfortable fact about artistic inspiration: that painters and poets often choose to make beauty out of trauma; that they might even be accused of exploiting the wound. Even the poem's title calls attention to the writing of poetry; it reminds us that a persona poem—a poem written in the voice of a character—is named for the oversized masks worn by the actors in ancient Greek theater.

Bachmann's "Mask" is evasive, as the wearing of masks so often allows us to be. The poem skitters emotionally, rhetorically, and even narratively. On the other hand, Daniel Garcia's "Reader, I Didn't Leave" appears initially to speak with great directness about domestic violence. The title—an allusion to the famous closing sentence of *Jane Eyre*—signals to readers that this will be a text about a seductive and abusive relationship.

Reader, I Didn't Leave

At first, I came back. *Stay with me—*
I did. Like summer rain

it was so fast. I had to start over.
A difference with rain & life

with him is: one had a sky to return
to after. The other took

hands to the face. I survived. This
also went against my wishes.

In eight short lines, Garcia presents the cycle of abuse. We begin with reconciliation. The speaker has returned after what has likely been a violent incident, an event so dangerous that the speaker was forced to leave in the first place. Almost immediately the seduction resumes as the lover coaxes, "*Stay with me*." This calm interlude lasts barely a full line before the unease increases and another abusive act occurs. "It was so fast," admits the speaker.

In fact, the poem moves so rapidly that a reader may find it difficult to remain oriented within the narrative. The poet uses short, clipped sentences, often forgoing transitions and explanatory phrases. We are forced to dart from declaration to declaration and to make our own meaning from this piecemeal summary of events. "The other took / hands to the face," muses the speaker; the most brutal passage in the poem has been made oblique. The violence is passive and disembodied. Garcia doesn't write *my face* but "the face." And "took / hands" transforms a slap or punch or pinch into an action without an actor. The lover's hands were separate from his body, detached from sentiment and the intention to hurt. By the final couplet, it's clear that the speaker has left the lover again. "I survived," Garcia writes. And then comes the poem's final blow—that survival itself went against the speaker's wishes, that they did not consent even to remaining alive.

Cathy Linh Che's "The German word for dream is traume" recounts the pain of sexual assault. Telling the story in three sections, the poet edges slowly toward trauma.

The German word for dream is traume.

The coal-dust hushed
parameters of the room.

Outside, my mother stitched
whole dresses for $3.00 a piece.

I slept in a bedroom
which faced the street.

A cheerleader was killed
in a drive-by that year.

She died in her sleep.

I watched the headlights
sweep overhead.

*

It felt like skin.

It did not
feel obscene.

When that boy
tongue-kissed me

and wiped
his mouth,

it was a coming
into knowledge.

*

When my mother whispered,
Has anyone touched you there?
I had to pick.

Alan, I said.

I was seven.
The training wheels
were coming off.

Between the couch
and wall, the ceiling was white
with popcorn bits. The boys stood

and watched. I lay there,
my eyes open like a doll's.
Someone said, *Let me try.*

He pulled down his pants
and rode on top,
then abruptly stopped.

The boys laughed,
said *Shhh*
and stood me up.

Holocaust survivor and essayist Jean Améry, writing about his experiences during World War II, observes, "Whoever has succumbed to torture can no longer feel at home in the world. The shame of destruction cannot be erased. Trust in the world, which already collapsed in part at the first blow, but in the end, under torture, fully, will not be regained." Once this trust in the order of things has been broken, the tortured are irrevocably altered.

I think of Cathy Linh Che's poem as a series of concentric circles; the speaker gradually approaches the incident that changed her forever, permanently annihilating her trust in the world. Each section forms a smaller, tighter ring around the trauma. In the first, the speaker—a very young girl—begins by setting the scene. We are placed in a bedroom. Somewhere nearby, a mother sews clothing at less than a living wage.

Next, we shift to the memory of a rape. The assault is wrenched almost completely away from a specific place or time. The violence floats. It is disembodied. And the poem's lines are tiny, disconcerting in their brevity.

Finally, in the longest section, the speaker offers specifics about what has happened. The poem's title reveals itself to have been a deliberate misdirection all along. The German word for dream is *Traum*. Its plural form is *Träume*. So, this piece contains many dreams or, rather, many nightmares. There are plural abuses. "I had to pick," the speaker says, when her mother asks, "Has anyone touched you there?" She chooses one name out of a group of boys who have assaulted her. She offers her mother one nightmare from a series of horrible dreams. The last thing the poem discloses is that, after the assaults, the boys stood the speaker up, as if returning her to a vertical position could erase or muffle their violence. As long as she is standing, their actions imply, the rapes must not have occurred. "Shhh," they tell her.

In fact, the poem does whisper. It speaks quietly in lines that read as nearly emotionless. But whispering is not the same as silence. She says, "Alan." She describes the boys. Through an oblique approach to trauma, the speaker finds a way to name what they did to her.

Writing Your Way In

1. Use the etymology of a word to explore trauma in a detached, cerebral voice. Imitate Beth Bachmann's approach in "Mask," picking a word that is both abstract and that is associated with real, concrete objects.
2. Tell a story of trauma in a brief, broken manner. Use quick, declarative sentences. Talk around, near to, above, and beneath the pain.
3. In the spirit of Cathy Linh Che's poem, mistranslate a word from another language. Through mistranslation, explore the complexity of trauma. Consider how trauma can be misunderstood both by those who have experienced the pain directly and by others around them.

CHAPTER 6

Fragmentations and Punctures

How does   break the stories we   ?

Sometimes trauma leaves gaps in our memories. The pain can pierce our understanding of the world, punch holes in our cherished notions of justice or stability or family. So, it makes sense that poems written in response to trauma should mirror these perforations. After trauma, we are often made incomplete, and the poem's task is to embody the hollows left behind.

In a sequence titled "Glossary of Grief," Julia Kolchinsky attempts to construct a lexicon of exile. The poems in this series are in conversation with the work of Ilya Kaminsky, a fellow Ukrainian Jewish American poet who, like Kolchinsky, often writes about the Shoah as well as the catastrophe of Soviet rule.

A glossary is a gathering of words or terms accompanied by definitions, explanations of meaning, or analyses of obscure expressions. Organized alphabetically, a glossary is like any list; we can form a story out of juxtaposition, the fortuitous placement of one term alongside another. We might also think of a glossary as an answer to the diasporic condition. By bringing together disparate pieces of language, the poet creates a community of speech, shared idioms, and words joined by ancestral roots.

With Kolchinsky's "Glossary / Глоссарий," it is the very word "glossary" that comes under scrutiny. A succession of associative fragments, the poem shows that the refugee exists in a state of tonguelessness, dispossessed from her first language.

Glossary / Глоссарий

"glistening smoothness, luster," probably
from Scandinavian because light
can only come from elsewhere
we can only come from somewhere
(Днепр *Dnepr* Дніпро *Dnipro*
from Sarmatian *Dānu apara* "river
on the far side" or from Scythian *Dānu apr*
"deep river" home river birth river tongue river
recollected river mouth river my river river
or else (compare Icelandic *glossi* "a spark, a flame,"
related to *glossa* "to flame") static fire kin
to its rage a kiln to what it hides or holds
noun to the act it carries hole to everything
it's missing a river to a river name
to obsolete Dutch *gloos* "a glowing" from
Middle High German *glos*; probably ultimately
from the same source as English *glow*
the tongue returns else-
where it's never been Late Latin *glossa*
"obsolete or foreign word" one that requires
explanation more words and light and rivers
from Greek *glōtta* (Attic) "language, a tongue"
literally "the tongue" (as the organ of speech)
as organ of song as *golos* голос
from Old Church Slavonic *glogu* "thorn"
voice vox our mouths river
our mouths sing stinging

When she was only six, Kolchinsky's family emigrated in 1993.

Jewish refugees, they left Dnipro, which, at the time, was still Dnepropetrovsk. This is a part of the world in which the names of cities are always changing, one name supplanted by another, depending on the current leader or how the borders have been redrawn by the latest empire.

In an interview, the poet explains the important role that Ukraine plays in her writing:

> Because I started writing at such a young age, when my identity as "immigrant" and "foreign" and "different" was most palpable and strongly reinforced by my peers and surroundings, it's almost inevitable that my poems both escape from and into an unknowable past in Ukraine and our flight away from it—a past so veiled and unremembered now that it bursts with imaginative potential.

"Glossary / Глоссарий" certainly enacts this conflict between an escape from Ukraine and a constant movement toward the remembered landscape of childhood. As the poem tries to define all the nuances of the word "glossary," pointing to different origins, Kolchinsky also begins to investigate the etymology of "Dnipro." She explains that the city comes "from Sarmatian *Dānu apara*," which means "river / on the far side." By pursuing the development of these words, the poet can articulate the particular idiom of her displacement; hers is a dialect of fragments, sharp as bits of river stone. The poem ends as it began—with disintegrated sentences. "Our mouths river," mourns the speaker, "our mouths sing   stinging."

James Allen Hall's "Inheritance at Corresponding Periods of Life, at Corresponding Seasons of the Year, as Limited by Sex" reads less like an entry in a glossary and more like a fractured inventory of biological facts about animals and human beings. The speaker offers snippets of information about frogs, bees, ponies; each curious detail and cold statistic allows the speaker to address their parents' intertwining dysfunctions.

Inheritance at Corresponding Periods of Life, at Corresponding Seasons of the Year, as Limited by Sex

Some species mate, then decapitate.
Some frogs never reproduce the same
place twice. Some species film with
fancy cameras their fucking. My father
said my mother requested one night
to be whipped by strangers. No species
lack pleasure receptors in their ears.
Some bees use sex as revenge, some
as memory. Fell ponies never uncouple.
Some sharks orgasm with their eyes
so can never trust their seeing. My father
said *I can't do it*, sent my brother inside
the porn store to buy what my mother
wanted. Some call out to a god, others
to excrement. I am not making equivalencies.
Finches sing to seduce. Ornithologists
theorize the same song also eulogizes
if produced in a tree hollow. That this is
not the saddest fact in all of zoology is
zoology's saddest fact. Unprompted,
my mother told me she loved my father
like a brother. Some mate for safety, to avoid
sadness, to self-flagellate. Some say *there,*
there as if pushing on a bruise. After
her affairs, my father forgave his wife.
For all species, desire is the most boring
verb, yet they connive for it most hours.
Some species of snake copulate in hopes
they are another species altogether. Grunion
bury their spawn in sand. My mother said
she would have aborted me, but the clinic

was closed. When whales abandon a grieving
mother, she does not find kindness again.
Some lives are taken down to salt, some to water.
Some species invent facts about the living
to explain the dead. I cannot fathom the bones
I find in the woods posed themselves like this,
though some species of grief find meaning
in minutia, a mechanism for survival. It is hard
to imagine a face for each skull.

"Inheritance at Corresponding Periods of Life, at Corresponding Seasons of the Year, as Limited by Sex" uses scientific factoids to create emotional detachment and narrative distance. Its tone is both wry and cynical. But beneath the speaker's coldness lies pain. They are deeply wounded by their parents' inability to love one another without causing injury in the process. These "species of grief," as Hall describes them, are depicted as a biological inevitability. The mother seems genetically programmed to wound the father through her voyeurism and sadism. She is equally vicious with her child, telling the speaker that "she would have aborted" them, "but the clinic / was closed."

The poem scurries, twitching between facts about the animal kingdom and truths of the small realm of family. The lines break at unexpected moments. "I am not making equivalencies," insists the speaker. The poem's fragmented form tells us otherwise. What the speaker learns from the maternal actions of snakes, grunions, and whales is a sort of Darwinian endurance, "a mechanism for survival" in the face of a mother's unbearable callousness. At the same time, the text recognizes that the brutality of a parent must come from somewhere, just as it's true some animals "mate for safety, to avoid / sadness, to self-flagellate." Such equivalencies make it possible for Hall to reflect on the entanglements of love and cruelty, the "saddest fact" of family.

Writing Your Way In

1. Write your own glossary of trauma. How does this pain mold your vocabulary? What words does it lead you to define? And what words are omitted?
2. As with James Allen Hall's "Inheritance at Corresponding Periods of Life, at Corresponding Seasons of the Year, as Limited by Sex" write a poem that incorporates scientific research to shed light on personal trauma. Create unexpected equivalencies.
3. Henri Raczymow—a French Jewish writer whose work often explores the intergenerational transmission of trauma—describes how traumatized memory is "shot through with holes." Write a draft in which trauma is recollected. Illustrate Raczymow's observation by incorporating holes—gaps that memory cannot fill in.

CHAPTER 7

Erasures

What is left behind after ████████*? What* █████ *remain?*

After a large-scale trauma, silence can descend like a thick, unreadable fog. The perpetrators try to conceal what they've done. They change their names. They disappear to other countries. The bystanders deny what they've seen. *We weren't there*, they say. Even the victims may participate in silence. Talking is too difficult. Speechlessness becomes a featherbed that cushions the body in softness.

Even when the trauma is of a more private variety—intimate partner violence, physical abuse—the same kind of quiet can emerge.

In the form known as an erasure, a poet removes or expunges parts of a text to produce a poem; the primary source might be a newspaper article, a public lecture, or a court record. A successful erasure makes audible what was smothered in the original material. And through the forceful gesture of wiping away words, the poet creates a space for muffled language to speak.

Reading erasures, I'm often reminded of how the state erases documents, altogether or in part. I am not alone in finding such oppressive echoes in the process of erasure. In an essay about the form, Solmaz Sharif—whose own collection *LOOK* employs the technique—writes,

> The first time I confronted erasure as an aesthetic tactic I was

horrified. I don't remember exactly when or what it was. I know I was in the United States. I know it was an erasure undertaken by a poet of the United States. I know it was after the invasions of Iraq and Afghanistan, after "extraordinary rendition" and disappeared men flown to secret sites in Somalia, certainly after attempted annihilation of indigenous languages and peoples, the enforced illiteracy of black slaves, certainly after Deir Yassin and the establishment, too, of this settler colonial nation. I know I thought of erasure as what a state does.

The government employee who censors documents is engaging in erasure. Redaction. Wite-Out. A pair of scissors snipping and snipping. Erasure as poetry contains this tradition while also inverting it. An erasure frequently reveals what isn't being said: suppressed truths and buried narratives. And so, it should come as no surprise that erasures often become political poems. Or, as writer Muriel Leung observes, "To make something new from these old bones will always be a political act, either to liberate the text from its original meaning or to reinscribe the violence in another form."

There are, of course, erasures of literary texts. Jen Bervin erases Shakespeare's sonnets in her book *Nets*. Janet Holmes disappears poems by Emily Dickinson throughout *The ms of m y kin*. In his collection *Radi Os*, Ronald Johnson vanishes *Paradise Lost*.

But, more frequently, erasures begin with bureaucratic documents. In her book *Zong!*, M. Nourbese Philip uses court records from the infamous insurance case of a British slave ship to examine the construction of narrative and its relationship to trauma. Srikanth Reddy's *Voyager* takes as its source material the rather pallid memoir of Kurt Waldheim, a former secretary-general of the United Nations and a man who denied both knowledge of and participation in Nazi war crimes. Philip Metres takes on the US military's Standard Operating Procedures to present the voices that were talked over or explicitly silenced during America's post-9/11 wars in the Middle East.

Tracy K. Smith's "Declaration" is an erasure of the United States Declaration of Independence, one of the most famous public pieces of writing in American history. Many readers likely know passages from the beginning of the text. "When in the course of human events." Or, perhaps, "We hold these truths to be self-evident." But Smith's erasure focuses on the list of "Facts . . . submitted to a candid world," a portion of the text that is perhaps less familiar to many.

Declaration

He has

sent hither swarms of Officers to harass our people

He has plundered our—

ravaged our—

destroyed the lives of our—

taking away our—

abolishing our most valuable—

and altering fundamentally the Forms of our—

In every stage of these Oppressions We have Petitioned for
Redress in the most humble terms:

Our repeated
Petitions have been answered only by repeated injury.

We have reminded them of the circumstances of our emigration
and settlement here.

—taken Captive

on the high Seas

to bear—

As an erasure, "Declaration" remains a document that calls for freedom. The text still focuses on restoration and reparation, just as its original source material does, but the voice has shifted. That first-person plural speaker no longer sounds like the fifty-six delegates of the Second Continental Congress. Instead, the *we* and *our* of Smith's poem are the enslaved people whose oppression the Founders not only overlooked but also facilitated. "Declaration" underscores a hard irony—that men like Thomas Jefferson could call for their own liberation from an abusive power without acknowledging how they themselves abused and subjugated others.

In Kiki Petrosino's poetry collection *White Blood*, the poet erases her own DNA results into verse, the lines airy and delicate. Petrosino's erasures reveal what's underneath the neutrality of scientific information. Each time the poet reinterprets or reinscribes the same page of her genetic results, a new response to the facts emerges.

Anyone who has ever taken a DNA test knows that pie charts and other types of data can flatten the violence of history. A few blobs of color on a map of the world cannot express the devastation of the Middle Passage. These are forced journeys. Someone is captured and shipped away. Someone else is sexually assaulted and compelled to give birth. Petrosino articulates the violence of her ancestors' history. She makes trauma visible again, although the dispassionate language of the DNA testing lingers.

In her novel *Beloved*, Toni Morrison transforms trauma into a furious spirit. It's an apparition that haunts the home of people who were once enslaved. The book's protagonist, Sethe, observes,

> Someday you be walking down the road and you hear something or see something going on. So clear. And you think it's you thinking it up. A thought picture. But no. It's when you bump into a rememory that belongs to somebody else. Where I was before I came here, that place is real. It's never going away. Even if the whole farm—every tree and blade of grass of it dies. The picture is still there and what's more, if you go there—you who never was there—if you go there and stand in the place where it was, it will happen again; it will be there, waiting for you. . . . Because even though it's all over—over and done with—it's going to always be there waiting for you.

Rememory is trauma that haunts. It troubles and revisits the body. It keeps returning. In Kiki Petrosino's erasures, a ghostly, white-gray alphabet drifts beneath the words of the poem. No matter how many times the DNA results are effaced and replaced with verse, the clinical voice of science (which has so frequently been used to assist in atrocity) resurfaces, spectral and persistent.

With Smith's and Petrosino's poems, the source materials seem in opposition to one another; the two texts have vastly different audiences and goals. One is arguably the most public document in American history. The other reveals the tiniest, most intimate details about the poet: her genetic information. But both speak to origin and birth. Through erasure, Smith and Petrosino are able to confront the American slave trade, unearthing the traumas that wait, respectively, beneath patriotic speech and medical data.

Writing Your Way In

1. Select a document that has a public function but to which you have an intimate and difficult connection. Erase portions of the text, writing a poem that speaks directly to the trauma you wish to explore.
2. Select a more private document that is connected to personal

history. For instance, this could be a letter written by an ancestor. Erase pieces of the text so that it articulates what was left silent or unspoken in the past.

3. Select a poem that you wrote based on one of the other exercises in this book. Erase parts of the draft, so that it now considers trauma in a new way. Surprise yourself. Uncover something—an idea, an image, a haunting—you didn't realize was present in the text.

CHAPTER 8

Surrealisms

When the poem dreams of trauma, what reality is discovered?

The surreal lies just above what we understand to be real. It is a painting of a desolate landscape in which clocks melt, timepieces draped over tree branches or dripping at the end of a platform. It is a film in which a beautiful woman walks down a dark hall, and the candelabras mounted on the walls are held by living hands that shift uneasily with the girl's movements. The surreal is a ballet where dancers twist like splashes of oil paint on a wild canvas.

As a cultural movement, surrealism developed after the end of World War I and was a way for artists to explore the unconscious mind, that place where dreams and nightmares intersect. Surrealism flourished during the interwar period. It makes sense that, in response to the horrors of war, many artists turned inward, toward the terrifying landscape of the psyche to make sense of what they had witnessed: trenches, shellshock, the devastation of no man's land.

The traumatized mind is often pursued by strangeness: alarming and surprising images, dreamlike visions, moments of reality that seem unreal. But it's not merely that trauma can, in some cases, cause hallucinations or radical breaks with reality. It's also that the causes of trauma are frequently so horrible as to seem entirely outside of what's true and factual. Extreme cruelty and violence resist the intellect. They defy comprehension. In such cases, surrealism may be the best way to represent the unintelligibility of trauma.

In her landmark anthology, *Against Forgetting: Twentieth-Century Poetry of Witness*, Carolyn Forché writes about what she calls "the poetry of witness," arguing that this form of verse "frequently resorts to paradox and difficult equivocation." Often, and particularly in oppressive regimes, the real can only be represented accurately through the surreal. "Fabulation, the writing of the blatantly fictitious, becomes the recourse of those who would describe the everyday."

Lucas Jorgensen's prose poem "The Bureau of Mercy" explores a summer of clinical depression by operating in a surrealist mode, as if to say that a severe mental-health crisis can only be evoked by turning to dreamlike scenes. The ordinary will not suffice. Instead, Jorgensen presents a sequence of increasingly violent animal deaths, so that it's difficult to tell the speaker's nightmares from his waking life. The whole poem is made uncanny by its setting, an administrative space dedicated to—of all things—pity and benevolence. The use of slashes within the prose poem's rectangular space inspires further feelings of discomfort. These slashes introduce line breaks were there should be none, an uneasy tension between syntax and line.

The Bureau of Mercy

The summer I started / Prozac was a massacre / at work. The glue traps / that captured grasshoppers / careless in their collateral. / First, a frog. Then, a gecko. / Eventually, a snake, / juvenile. He writhed / against the trap, worked / himself deeper / and deeper / into the glue, spread / himself thin until / each inch of trap / held a leopard scale. His skin / like a tarp pulled taut / over his skeleton, leaving / no space to squirm / against it. I thought of myself, / once pinned down / by something so large / it was alien, like trying / to describe a flower /

> from another nature's world. I / picked up the strip of paper, / filled the bucket, dropped / the snake inside. My thoughts / plinked into the water / beside it. I was / guiltless. The snake / needed to drown.

It's unclear whether the speaker is experiencing trauma-related depression, but the gluey deaths of the animals certainly feel traumatic in themselves. Jorgensen walks the reader through a progression, moving from trapped grasshoppers to frog to gecko to snake; with each murder, the dead creatures grow, becoming larger and more menacing. They are prophetic, almost reminiscent of Biblical plagues. And just as we arrive at the greatest of these deaths—that of the snake—the speaker recalls a time he was "once pinned down / by something so large / it was alien." This memory might be a nightmare or a symbol of depression's crushing pain, despair made animate, voracious.

The poem ends with a terrifying and ambiguous image. In the final few sentences, it is evident that the speaker now identifies with all the creatures who have been caught in the glue trap and particularly with the serpent. "My thoughts / plinked into the water / beside it," he observes. When the speaker concludes that "The snake / needed to drown," it's hard to know if this final gesture stands for self-preservation or self-destruction, a killing of the self. It's also difficult to tell if the speaker truly believes that the snake had to die or if he is simply tamping down feelings of guilt. "I was / guiltless," says the speaker, although no one has accused him. The trauma is inside him, and only he can drown the hurt.

Lindsay Lusby's "Self-Portrait as Psychopomp" turns to surrealism as a means of expressing the inexpressible parts of trauma. The poem is about a grown child's effort to speak with her dying father about end-of-life care. But as soon as the father begins to respond to this painful question, the narrative becomes horrifying. The conversation is so unbearable that the speaker can only communicate through an otherworldly vernacular.

Self-Portrait as Psychopomp

when we ask my father how / he wants to die / he opens his mouth and the crows / and the crows / and the crows flash their purple-black / feathers over his bed / bastard birds named breathless / named hunger named / sleep named something rotten in the fatherless / scavengers plucking at the bones / and the bones / and the bones still sunken under / skin sunken under air too heavy / to swim up through / he says / *don't you know we live at the bottom / of an ocean named sky* / we do and we / do and we don't know how / to hold this in our barbed grasp / without breaking the glass globe / of his dreaming he says / *look at these clouds like seafoam / floating on currents of troposphere* / and the crows darken the air / in the rooms where they wait / and they wait and / we wait for him to / close his heavy eyes

Like "The Bureau of Mercy," "Self-Portrait as Psychopomp" is a prose poem punctuated with slashes, a technique that introduces the serrated sensation of line breaks into non-lineated verse. But that's where the similarities end. Jorgensen's sentences are steady and declarative; the speaker is disturbed by the experience of working in the Bureau of Mercy, but he isn't unmoored. Lusby's poem, on the other hand, is breathless, its syntax fractured. The speaker seems to be grasping—and gasping—for the next image, each new idea delirious and unnerving.

A psychopomp is a mythological creature whose job is to shuttle the recently dead to the underworld or to the afterlife. By framing the poem as a self-portrait, Lusby argues that the speaker is responsible for guiding her father to and beyond death. She wears the myth of the psychopomp like a mask; disguised, she can speak about her guilt and shame. Like the crows that "darken the air," the speaker too waits for her father to "close his heavy eyes." Horrifically, she sees herself as a carrion bird, a scavenger hunched in the road, her curved beak "plucking at the bones." The poem carries these anxieties and doesn't attempt to resolve them. Instead, we are left to understand that this poem hasn't allowed the speaker to find any closure. She will always be in that room, unable to leave behind that swirling memory of her father in his final days.

Some traumas are so devastating that the mind must develop an entirely new set of images to describe what has happened. A poem like "Self-Portrait as Psychopomp" asks, What if only the language of nightmares can convey the experience? What if the poem insists that we, the readers, enter that terrifying dreamscape?

Writing Your Way In

1. In the way of "The Bureau of Mercy," write a draft that includes a sequence of surrealist images that progress, one following the other, perhaps increasing in size, threat, or terror as they go.
2. Write a self-portrait in which the speaker is depicted as a mythological creature. How does this character respond to trauma? How does this character shoulder the burdens of that pain?
3. Write a draft that contains surreal imagery to explore trauma's uncanniness, its devastating effect on the body and mind. Try to include at least six surreal images in the poem.

CHAPTER 9

Nonlinearities

What if we start with the middle, then move to the end, then go back to the start?

Trauma wounds our psyches. But it also injures our confidence in the solidity of narrative. To tell a story in straight lines—*first this happened, then this, and finally this*—no longer makes sense in a life that has been overturned. A story structured like a pyramid, with its rising and falling actions, its denouement, is too well-behaved for trauma. After all, trauma is seldom so easily divided into obedient peaks and valleys. It refuses exposition, much less a tidy resolution.

"The time is out of joint," Hamlet famously says after learning that his uncle murdered his father. It's shocking, dizzying information. The young prince's response implies that, after trauma, time is like a dislocated shoulder that needs to be pushed back into place. Without treatment, time will bruise; it will continue to swell or dislodge.

I'm reminded of Jorge Semprum's novel, *The Long Voyage*, which is set largely on a train that is moving toward the Buchenwald concentration camp. The journey of the locomotive suggests one possible form of storytelling: linear and traveling toward a fixed destination.

But the narrator of *The Long Voyage* has a mind that journeys in all directions. His thoughts circle, spiral, move forward and back. Trapped in the boxcar, his body is carried toward an unbearable ending point. And in reaction, his mind twists out and away.

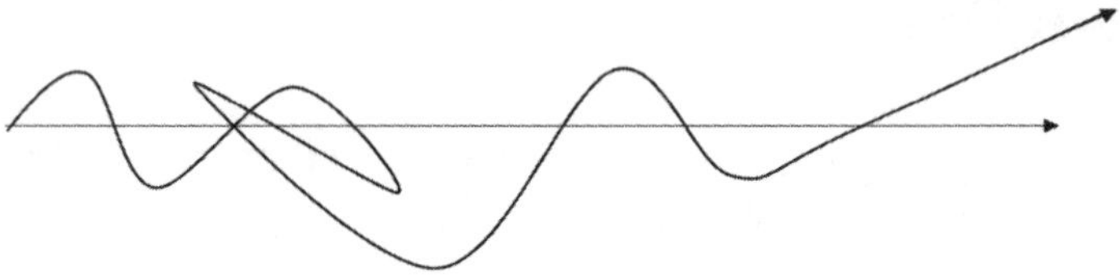

In poems that engage with trauma we often see a resistance to continuity. Beginnings, middles, and endings are often jumbled, shaken out of their usual order. Straight lines speak to stability, directness, stories that have rules. But trauma is all blur and ambiguity, a world destabilized. It's fitting that many poems of trauma reflect this breakdown of narrative and reveal a distrust of linear storytelling.

In Allison Benis White's "Description of Symptoms," the poet's handling of white space and asterisks—which are often used to convey the omission of letters or words from a text—conveys inchoate grief. Divided into five sections, five tiny scenes, the piece feels disjointed, as if the speaker herself were a collage of bereavement, her psyche like pieces of torn paper that have been glued together.

Description of Symptoms

Now my hands buried
in my hair, resting on piano keys
in the back of my head.
This is the music I am playing
through my mind: a dark room singing
a song that will not have children.

*

Lying on the floor tonight, snowflakes
cut from paper laid over my eyes, a hand
carved from wood laid over my mouth.
If the truth is the thing you must not say,
I will speak for the vase now
as it falls: it is better never
to be at all.
*
A hand on the back of my head
made of glass, my love, my eyes,
filled with wire, life. Once
I watched a bird's shadow cross a field
in the wind: a black hat that could not stop
tumbling. My eyes are sore
from seeing, my lips from speaking.
*
How a ribbon curls when pulled
across a scissor's blade, I am practicing
transformation, pain. How the dark hair
of imagination, uncut, grows down
to the floor. What is left
but to make a world, a war?
*
Or a landscape in which to stay alive
(ghost flower/house of breath). Another wish: language
drilled through ice, through my life.
If grief is love with nowhere to go, this is
my mouth turning into snow.
This is somewhere.

Allison Benis White has said of her poem that it "was written after filling out medical intake forms for a doctor's appointment last year.

I was grieving for a friend who had ended her life, and I was experiencing symptoms I could not quite articulate." While the poem's title feels clinical, the language of the poem is electric with sensation and emotion. The speaker attempts to develop a sequence of metaphors, figures of speech that will allow her to accept the friend's decision to die by suicide. In one instance, she imagines "a song that will not have children." In another, she conceives of a "vase now / as it falls: it is better never / to be at all." And although the poem's narrative is fragmented and nonlinear, the voice of the speaker is entirely cohesive in mourning.

While "Description of Symptoms" addresses a terrible and private loss, Franny Choi's "The World Keeps Ending, and the World Goes On" experiments with time to examine a series of cataclysmic events, a cascade of wide-scale, global traumas.

The World Keeps Ending, and the World Goes On

Before the apocalypse, there was the apocalypse of boats:
boats of prisoners, boats cracking under sky-iron, boats making
corpses
bloom like algae on the shore. Before the apocalypse, there was the
apocalypse
of the bombed mosque. There was the apocalypse of the taxi driver
warped
by flame. There was the apocalypse of the leaving, and the having
left—
of my mother unsticking herself from her mother's grave as the
plane
barreled down the runway. Before the apocalypse, there was the
apocalypse
of planes. There was the apocalypse of pipelines legislating their
way
through sacred water, and the apocalypse of the dogs. Before which
was

the apocalypse of the dogs and the hoses. Before which, the apocalypse
of dogs and slave catchers whose faces glowed by lantern-light.
Before the apocalypse, the apocalypse of bees. The apocalypse of buses.
Border fence apocalypse. Coat hanger apocalypse. Apocalypse in
the textbooks' selective silences. There was the apocalypse of the settlement
and the soda machine; the apocalypse of the settlement and
the jars of scalps; there was the bedlam of the cannery; the radioactive rain;
the chairless martyr demanding a name. I was born from an apocalypse
and have come to tell you what I know—which is that the apocalypse began
when Columbus praised God and lowered his anchor. It began when a continent
was drawn into cutlets. It began when Kublai Khan told Marco, *Begin*
at the beginning. By the time the apocalypse began, the world had already
ended. It ended every day for a century or two. It ended, and another ending
world spun in its place. It ended, and we woke up and ordered Greek coffees,
drew the hot liquid through our teeth, as everywhere, the apocalypse rumbled,
the apocalypse remembered, our dear, beloved apocalypse—it drifted
slowly from the trees all around us, so loud we stopped hearing it.

Initially, the poem moves backward, each catastrophe preceded by another, so that it feels as if we're traveling back in time, attempting to locate the original trauma at the start of human history.

But almost as soon as this retroactive pattern is established, the poet shifts the text's focus. The speaker begins to describe her mother "unsticking herself from her mother's grave." From there, the piece slides rapidly between political and ecological apocalypses, disastrous moments in history, such as when Columbus "lowered his anchor" in the Americas. Occasionally, we return to the personal. "I was born from an apocalypse / and have come to tell you what I know," the speaker explains. Time is destabilized. The world tilts chaotically on its axis. In long, tumbling lines the poem cycles through dozens of apocalypses. The language is breathless. It wheezes and rushes on. Meanwhile, each destruction rips apart the world while tearing too at our own small lives.

Writing Your Way In

1. Turn the trauma you wish to explore into a sequence of tiny, discrete scenes, each one operating independently of the others. Disrupt time. Allow each section of the draft to move independently of the others. If the poem finds any sort of cohesion, let it be through the use of linked images rather than through the construction of a linear narrative.
2. Write a draft with long, cyclical lines. Let the syntax of the draft convey the overwhelming, exhausting nature of trauma.
3. Keeping Jorge Semprun's *The Long Voyage* in mind, write a poem that moves back and forth from linear to nonlinear narrative. To represent the linear element of the draft, you may want to use an emblem such as a highway, a road, or a train track—something that travels in an unbroken, direct line.

CHAPTER 10

Counterfactual Histories and Alternate Universes

Why do we imagine histories that undo our own? Why do we visit other universes?

After trauma, many people want to erase their pain as if the hurt were an Etch a Sketch—give it a good shake, and the aluminum powder settles once again into a perfect blankness. When a poem constructs a counterfactual history, the writer obliterates the past and draws new lines over it, offering the reader a fresh narrative. The poet asks, *What if?* And the poem is an answer to that hypothetical.

A poem built on the conceit of an alternate universe reinvents narrative to change not only what has already occurred but the present and future as well. Poems that posit alternate universes work on a larger scale than do counterfactual histories—after all, we're talking about the creation of an entire cosmos.

In a counterfactual history, the past is simply replaced. In an alternate universe, we might envision a second universe positioned alongside the first, so that the reader senses both, running side by side like the parallel lines of a train track. The two universes coexist. The first is filled with trauma, and the second is unwounded, if barely for the length of the poem.

Alternate universes might seem the stuff of speculative or

science fiction. But doesn't trauma often split the psyche into multiple dimensions? The loop of being trapped inside trauma can resemble time travel. Before-trauma and after-trauma are like discrete points stretched far apart, positioned in separate galaxies. Only a wormhole could allow the mind to journey between these two distant locations.

It's such a human impulse: to envision bodies and places and even eras rendered untraumatized. Of course, we should we want to undo what is awful and unbearable. We want to imagine the worst could be otherwise. In Clint Smith's "Counterfactual," a grown speaker recalls a moment from childhood in which his father must end the boy's innocence to protect his son from the racism of the larger world.

Counterfactual

One night
when I was twelve years old
on a field trip some place
I can't remember, my friends
and I bought supersoakers

and turned the hotel parking lot
into our arena of saturation.
We hid behind cars
running through the darkness
that lay between the streetlights.
Seditious laughter ubiquitous
across the pavement.

Within ten minutes
my father came outside
grabbed me by the forearm
and led me inside to our room
with an unfamiliar grip.

Before I could invoke objection,
acquaint him with how foolish
he had made me look in front
of my friends,
he derided me for being so naïve.

Told me I couldn't be out here
acting the same as these white boys—
can't be pretending to shoot guns
can't be running in the dark
can't be hiding behind anything
other than your own teeth.

I know now how scared
he must have been,
how easily I could have fallen
into the obsolescence of the night.
That some man would mistake
this water for a good reason
to wash all of this away.

There are two counterfactual examples in this poem. The piece opens with a scene in which a Black child plays with his white friends, all of them holding water guns and running through the dark. They remain safe and unthreatened. Their games are joyful. The Black child is permitted his childhood; he is not made to feel that his existence is a hazard. He is allowed the same easy happiness as his white friends.

But then this tender *what if* is interrupted. The father hurries to his son and pulls him indoors to warn him of the terrible risks of such games. His words are urgent, sharpened by fear. In an interview, Smith explains:

A lot of the poem "Counterfactual" was about the pedagogy of

> black parenting, and the conversations that black parents have to have with their kids about growing up in a world that is taught to fear you. How you straddle that line between ensuring that your children are not naively navigating the world, and understanding that the things they do might have very different implications for them than they do for their non-black friends, but then also ensuring that your child knows it's not their fault, that there's nothing they've done to deserve such a caricature.

The poem ends with a second counterfactual history, so brief it's barely a flash of *what if*. This time, the speaker is imagined dying in "the obsolescence of the night." The closing lines of the poem wash away this appalling possibility that the speaker could have been killed for holding a plastic water gun. The water also functions as a baptism into grief. It brings the little boy closer to adult knowledge: that the world is dangerous for a Black child, that his body is viewed by others—especially figures in authority, those who have power to hurt him—as menacing, that he must do everything possible to avoid their intolerant gaze.

In Rhina Espaillat's "Suppose," the poet creates a tiny portrait of loss. A widow mourns her husband's death and slowly, methodically, begins to postulate an alternate universe in which they could be reunited. An Elizabethan sonnet, the poem follows all the conventions of the form. For instance, it explores mortality and love, two traditional concerns of the sonnet. The poet is also meticulous in her application of the rhyme scheme (*abab cdcd efef gg*). There's a clear rhetorical turn—what is called the *volta*—following the eighth line. And "Suppose" closes with a couplet whose simple music pairs perfectly with a devasting image of someone left both hopeful and hopeless by grief.

Suppose

A gift from physics: fantasy that rains
on the parched hours of my widowed night.
Suppose it's true the stream of time contains
each moment, as if holographed in light
whose speed preserves intact what used to be.
Suppose I calculate that speed and race
toward inches from our youth, and carefully
insert myself precisely in time-space
we spent together, close enough this side
of childhood, so as not to risk a drop
of change or separation by too wide
a gap. No random leap; no curious stop
at some mistaken lifetime that lacks you.
An idle hope. But it will have to do.

"Suppose" is preoccupied with the intersection of "fantasy" and what Espaillat calls a "gift from physics." The poem vibrates with images of movement, particles shifting, holographic glimmers. As if she were a mathematician of trauma, the speaker calculates the speed of light, hoping to arrive at the correct computations so that she can insert herself into a "time-space"—a where and a when—early on in her marriage. If she could only make physics serve her grief, then she might be able to avoid entirely this "mistaken lifetime" of widowhood.

The poem's self-restraint, its exquisite control of form, mirrors the speaker's stoicism. Throughout the sonnet, Espaillat moves with absolute certainty. The speaker knows reality should be otherwise; this parallel universe should be possible to reach. Suppose,

suppose, she keeps insisting. The text's rhythms embody the widow's thoughts as she postulates a world in which her husband might still be alive. "An idle hope," the poem closes, "But it will have to do." Readers can feel that moment in which the speaker leaves fantasy behind; that shift is palpable in the pause that follows the word "hope." Espaillat applies the artifice of iambic pentameter with great skill to dramatize the speaker's longing to remain in a "time-space" where she is not divided from her husband, their marriage undisturbed by death.

As Smith and Espaillat teach us, counterfactual histories and alternate universes are shaky constructions. Inevitably, the illusion of *what if* shatters like a storefront window struck with a stone. Language offers a temporary reprieve. Then poem the ends. And we must reenter the pain.

Writing Your Way In

1. Imitating Clint Smith's approach in "Counterfactual," write a draft that introduces a counterfactual history. Over the course of the poem, the speaker should learn (or be taught) a lesson. Once the speaker has acquired this knowledge, is it possible to return to innocence?
2. Write a poem set in an alternate universe. How long can you keep the parallel worlds separate? What happens as the trauma enters your newly imagined cosmos?
3. Using what you learned in chapter 2, "Repetitions," write a poem that asks *what if*, over and over. Keep offering new hypotheses about how trauma might be escaped, avoided, or erased. Invent as many counterfactual histories as you can. Let the poem exhaust itself with these efforts to invent different possibilities for the past.

CHAPTER 11

Rewindings and Restorations

What if we can undo the trauma, at least for the length of a poem?

Sometimes, the traumatized don't need to venture into other universes. Our poems can stay right here on this planet and still find ways to undo the terrible. A common symptom of trauma is to replay the devastating event in one's thoughts. Trauma is like a cassette tape. We spool it backward and then restart the narrative. So, what if a poem could simply rewind the pain? What if the poem stops right before the trauma begins and the speaker concludes with happiness instead of grief?

Martin Amis's novel *Time's Arrow* tells the story of a Nazi doctor's life in reverse, beginning with his death and ending with his birth. Given how medicine was corrupted and defiled under Nazi rule, it's only by playing the physician's life backward that his actions appear moral. At Auschwitz, the murders he commits in the name of Nazi science—all those grim violations of his Hippocratic oath—become life-saving measures: "A shockingly inflamed eyeball at once rectified by a single injection. Innumerable ovaries and testes seamlessly grafted into place. Women went out of that lab looking 20 years younger." As reviewer Michiko Kakutani has said, "Amis creates a devastatingly specific portrait of the Nazis' warped mentality: only in a completely upside-down, backward world, he suggests, are their actions comprehensible."

Many forms of trauma feel like this; they cannot be understood except when inverted. They are manageable if—for the duration of the poem—they never happened at all. As with *Time's Arrow*, Matt Rasmussen's "Reverse Suicide" rewinds as a way of refiguring an unbearable event: in this case, the death of a brother.

Reverse Suicide

The guy Dad sold your car to
comes back to get his money,

leaves the car. With filthy rags
we rub it down until it doesn't shine

and wipe your blood into
the seams of the seat.

Each snowflake stirs before
lifting into the sky as I

learn you won't be dead.
The unsuffering ends

when the mess of your head
pulls together around

a bullet in your mouth.
You spit it into Dad's gun

before arriving in the driveway
while the evening brightens

and we pour bag after bag
of leaves on the lawn,

waiting for them to leap
onto the bare branches.

With "Reverse Suicide," self-annihilation transforms into creation. Death becomes life. Blood is unhemorrhaged. Told backward, the most horrific images in the poem are made surreal and even beautiful. The brother's head seals shut, now whole again. He spits a bullet into his father's gun. The poem closes with a lovely domestic scene: raked leaves "leap / onto the bare branches" of trees, so that even the natural, autumnal world resides in a state before death, almost prelapsarian.

Ross Gay's "A Small Needful Fact" is about Eric Garner, a Black man murdered by a police officer in 2014. The text focuses on Garner's work for the Parks and Recreation Horticultural Department. Garner's death is pushed out of the poem, although a few disturbing echoes remain.

A Small Needful Fact

Is that Eric Garner worked
for some time for the Parks and Rec.
Horticultural Department, which means,
perhaps, that with his very large hands,
perhaps, in all likelihood,
he put gently into the earth
some plants which, most likely,
some of them, in all likelihood,
continue to grow, continue
to do what such plants do, like house
and feed small and necessary creatures,
like being pleasant to touch and smell,

like converting sunlight
into food, like making it easier
for us to breathe.

As Rassmussen does with his brother, Gay restores Garner to wholeness. For a moment, Eric Garner is un-murdered. Violence is palpably absent from the poem. We are shown his "very large hands" putting "gently into the earth / some plants." We learn how these green things continue to root in the soil long after Garner's murder. The plants house and feed "small creatures," making it easier, the poem ends, "for us to breathe."

That final word—"breathe"—is the closest Gay comes to addressing how a police officered killed Garner by suffocating him in a choke hold on a public sidewalk. Garner's last words were, "I can't breathe." Here, breath is Garner's gift. His work with the Parks and Recreation Horticultural Department allows "all of us to breathe," the poem explains. These are the poem's necessary facts—what we need to remember about the man.

The language of "A Small Needful Fact" is quiet and delicate. The text treats Garner's body with tenderness, and his own movements are loving. This is a man who cares about the earth and who believes in the vital work each of us can do with our hands. Whatever anxiety a reader might feel when encountering the name Eric Garner in the opening line—the worry that we are about to read a gruesome reenactment of murder—dissipates as the poem carefully, cautiously makes its argument. The poem is one long sentence. If you read the piece out loud, it's possible to recite the whole thing in one breath. But just barely.

Poems like "Reverse Suicide" and "A Small Needful Fact" underscore how often, in the face of trauma, we wish we had the power to undo the past. We can insist that our poems become sites of fleeting grace. We can assert the right to joy. In the brief space of the poem, we can unravel or push out the trauma. We can allow, however temporarily, the possibility of defiant, life-affirming alternatives to the pain.

Writing Your Way In

1. Tell a trauma narrative backward. In rewinding the story, how do you transform the pain? How do ordinary images of trauma become surreal (or even positive) when played in reverse?
2. Imitate Ross Gay's approach in "A Small Needful Fact." Write a draft in which trauma is kept (almost) entirely out of the poem. Only allow the trauma to exist as a faint echo, an absence that is present.

CHAPTER 12

Archives and Testimonies

Where do we go when we enter the archive?
Where do we go when we enter the words of others?

In an earlier chapter, I write, "Many poems about trauma aren't really *about* the trauma itself. Instead, their primary purpose is to represent the traumatized mind—the fracturing of thought, how the intellect tries to piece the broken world back together." And, so far, we've looked mostly at poems whose purpose is mimetic. That is, their primary task is to mirror trauma's effects on our thinking and on our psyches. Form echoes content. Or, perhaps, content walks in the shadow of form.

However, there are poems whose main duty is to tell a story and to make an argument about that story; to insist: *this trauma occurred*. Often such poems resist lyricism and lean heavily on narrative techniques, as their primary function is to communicate information and convey historical facts. They are documentation. They are police reports. They are dispatches sent from the front. They are artifacts pulled from rubble.

The archive—as a site of research and scholarship—can be one of the spaces in which such poems begin. But spending time in an archive isn't easy. It involves handling ugly, clunky, and important information. Perhaps, the research is collected in a dusty room. Maybe the poet sits at a long wooden table for hours, leaning over charts and barely legible documents. Maybe the work is boring or it disappoints. Maybe the poet doesn't find the answers she's looking for in those stacks.

There's a technical challenge to this process too. The difficult (often tedious) work of the researcher rubs up against the more imaginative task of making a poem. The archive makes its presence known. It can be an obstruction. It can be a labyrinth in which the poet loses herself. This is why, when we use research to write about trauma, the archive itself so often becomes a site of drama and friction. It can even become another character in the poem.

After all, archives are spaces of inclusion and exclusion. Archives speak. But they can remain obstinately silent as well. The archive is a product of a curator's whims, biases,limitations. Governments may decide what the archive retains and what it discards. The archive is subjective. Once, I wrote an essay about Markus Meyer, my great-grandfather, who was murdered in the Shoah. In my search to learn how he died, I found that the archive presented me with more questions than answers. I learned the date of his death. I learned where he died. But how? I never unearthed that fact. The closest I came to knowing was a scanned document that listed his name and an illegible cause of death. As a result, my essay had two duties. I had to acknowledge what was incomplete in the narrative, and I also had to try filling in the absences with lyric, elegiac language.

Layli Long Soldier's "38" tells the story of the thirty-eight Dakota men who were publicly executed—hanged—in Mankato, Minnesota, on December 26, 1862. This long prose poem is deeply researched, despite the fact that the speaker reminds us she isn't trained as a historian. The piece points to its struggles: how and where to start the story, how not to lose oneself on the broken path of narrative. The poem is indeed *about* a very specific and real historical trauma, but it is just as much about the technical challenges of recounting trauma, especially when that history has been erased by a government.

The closing sentences of the poem reenact the murders of the Dakota 38. Long Soldier's language swings out across the page, like a body hanging. But the last two lines feel like a moment of liberation from death. Rather than coming to rest in stillness, it as if the thirty-eight men are allowed finally to leap from the platform and to move beyond trauma.

We might, perhaps, picture them running through the grasses—grasses that are no longer a symbol of starvation but of release. The speaker argues that the poem is not a work of creativity. And yet, the whole text—with its nonlinear narrative, its self-reflective gestures, and its analysis of its own inventive processes—demonstrates the ways a poet marries the archive to imagination.

An archive isn't always housed in a building. Sometimes it's found outdoors at a site where atrocity occurred. Landscape becomes a memorial. The ground is a repository of trauma. In Peter Balakian's long poem, "Ozone Journal," a speaker describes the experience of excavating the bones of murdered Armenians in the Syrian desert. Like a photograph placed in a bath of developer solution, the geography is imprinted with stark images of genocide.

42.

At the caves.
M. is obsessed with light flickering down—
affect of the punctum:

while remaining a detail, the space fills up the whole picture.
M: *Were thousands of Armenians stuffed in here?*
B: *Fisk called them primitive gas chambers.*

M. drops the boom mic into darkness; sand floats through the light-chipped space.

If you tried to imagine death here, the detail is not the whole—the whole disappears.
The cave is a black gullet swallowing itself—

Accompanied by a camera crew, the speaker stands in a cave. The composition of the "light flickering down" is so striking that the stony space already feels as if it has been transformed into a photograph. The scene contains a *punctum*, a concept that comes from philosopher Roland Barthes's *Camera Lucida*. The punctum is the "element which rises from the scene, shoots out of it like an arrow, and pierces me." It is the one detail in a photograph that punctures the viewer; it is an image's central source of beauty and pain.

Alongside this meditation on art and artifice, Balakian places a moment of dialogue that sounds inartful but also accurate. Having spent a lot of time at sites of genocide myself, I find the conversation between M. and B. entirely plausible. Confronted by the horror and the unnerving stillness of the landscape, it can be difficult not to speak, not to break the silence with prosaic observations. How else to stop from weeping? How else to stay focused on the painful work of documentation?

At the end of this section, the speaker acknowledges that "the detail" of the cave "is not the whole—the whole disappears." The cave resembles an image of the ouroboros, a serpent swallowing its own tail. It's an infinite loop of catastrophe. The mind can neither escape the cave nor fully comprehend what happened there.

This is the problem with an act of violence as large as the Armenian genocide. We can only take in one detail at a time, one site of devastation and then another. But these pieces do not add up to a complete understanding of the event. The whole remains elusive. Or it vanishes altogether. In this way, Balakian is also critiquing the form of his poem. "Ozone Journal" has fifty-four parts, each section providing the reader with a new detail of the horror. But what do all those parts amount to? Not the whole brutality, Balakian seems to say.

An archive too may reside within a body, held there until it is spoken as story, which we call testimony. Poems grounded in firsthand testimony pose many of the same challenges as do those created by the archive. How do we sort through all the materials? How do we identify the seeds of a poem within the dry information? How do we find a balance between history—the importance of getting our facts right—and art? Taking the testimony of someone who has endured trauma is a skill that requires training and instruction. The USC Shoah Foundation, for instance, provides extensive guidelines to its interviewers, including how to prepare before an interview, what kind of research to perform, what to expect during the interview, and how to complete post-interview steps. "If the interviewee perceives you as unprepared or lacking knowledge," the guidebook warns, "they may shut down and not share the full dimensions of their experiences."

The word *testimony* shares etymological roots with *testament*. Both come from the same root, *testis*, meaning "witness." The Latin American narrative form of *testimonio* was developed by writer and ethnographer Miguel Barnet. In a work of testimonio, someone who has endured trauma and marginalization offers a first-person account of their own life. This story is recorded, and the interviewer—a writer—then transforms or molds the taped narration into literature, sometimes introducing fictional or even speculative elements while preserving the essential truths of the testimony.

Emily Jungmin Yoon's book *A Cruelty Special to Our Species* may be understood as extending the narrative approach of testimonio. To write her collection, Yoon began with testimonies gathered by earlier scholars to write about the experiences of Korean women who were forced into sexual slavery by the Imperial Japanese Army during World War II and were euphemistically called "Comfort Women."

In an interview, Yoon describes the process of writing *A Cruelty Special to Our Species*, and it's evident that the work required the poet to look carefully at her own methods:

> The people who went through the colonial period and the Korean War and everything that came after, the bloody history of Korea, they're all still alive and their stories are still being found. I'm the one who inherited them. Thinking about what that inherited

> trauma is and how I'm going to go back to talk about their history, it's always a complicated question. I'm always going to wonder what the best way for me to talk about them is. I think the poems were kind of born out of that struggle. I do believe that every poem is a question rather than a solution.

It seems right that this kind of poetry should come as a "struggle." These are difficult pieces about difficult history. With such poems, Yoon transforms testimony into a form of witness that has a cruel, compressed lyricism.

In an analysis of the Fortunoff Video Archive for Holocaust Testimonies at Yale University, clinical psychiatrist Dori Laub writes,

> To a certain extent, the interviewer-listener takes on the responsibility for bearing witness that previously the narrator felt he bore alone, and therefore could not carry out. It is the encounter and the coming together between the survivor and listener, which makes possible something like a repossession of the act of witnessing. This joint responsibility is the source of the reemerging truth.

I would argue that poems based on testimony create a similar dynamic. Whether you choose to collect an oral history yourself or decide to follow Yoon's approach, the poet becomes a second interviewer-listener. The poem gives lyric form to an encounter between speech and hearing. It causes too "a repossession of the act of witnessing."

Many of Yoon's poems move jaggedly across the page, visibly broken. She inserts spaces into the text or else deletes them to create pauses and hesitations that become not only visible but also audible to the reader. Reading *A Cruelty Special to Our Species*, I'm reminded of Hannah Arendt's pronouncement in *Eichmann in Jerusalem: A Report on the Banality of Evil*: "The holes of oblivion do not exist. Nothing human is that perfect, and there are simply too many people in the world to make oblivion possible. One man will always be left alive to tell the story." In many of Yoon's poem, a woman has been left alive. She tells her story in prose. And Yoon translates this testimony into punctured, perforated verse.

Writing Your Way In

1. Write a prose poem that incorporates a large amount of research. Address your own narrative decisions in the draft. Point to the ways in which trauma strains the limits of your language.
2. Write a draft about your experiences in the archive. Describe the experience of searching for information, of looking through databases, of handling artifacts or fragile documents. What did you learn? What did you fail to discover? How is use of the archive a rhetorical strategy—a way of making an argument about fact or historical truth?
3. Imitating Peter Balakian's strategy, write a poem that contains at least ten sections. Set the poem in a site that signifies or that bore witness to the trauma you wish to explore. Include vivid descriptions of the setting. Include dialogue.
4. Write two poems or, maybe, a poem in two parts:
    a. The first piece should be based on testimony. You can perform an interview yourself or you can use previously collected testimony.
    b. Write a companion piece in which you analyze the challenges, uncertainties, and nuances of using testimony.

CHAPTER 13

Ekphrasis

How do we contemplate pain as if it were a painting displayed on a wall?

Sometimes, in writing about trauma, we may wish to stand at a distance and regard the pain with the detachment of a curator in an art gallery. *Won't you stand next to me*, the poem might say to the reader. *Let us look up this interesting hurt and see what we make of it.*

With ekphrasis writing, we begin by describing a piece of art. This could be a painting, a sculpture, a photograph, a still frame, or even a scene from a film; ekphrastic writing can also discuss music or dance. Description then leads to discovery. When we need critical distance, if we wish to speak about trauma from a cooler, more clinical place, ekphrasis allows us a rhetorical structure—precise description followed by insight—that, by its very nature, allows for detachment. In stepping back to study a work of art, we inevitably step back (as if we ourselves are paintings or marble sculptures) to scrutinize the self.

Writing about what he calls "the emblem structure," scholar Michael Theune characterizes the form as working in two parts; it "begins with an organized description of an object and culminates with a meditation on that same object. In this way, the emblem structure moves from sight to insight, from perception to reflection." Theune is interested in the rhetorical forms that poems can take; ekphrasis, for example, advocates for an encounter with the self that begins with an object beyond the self. It's true that we can pour a poem into the shape of a sonnet or a villanelle. But we can also view argument as a form, one that follows its own conventions and predetermined structure. And because ekphrastic poems start with descriptive passages before transforming into encounters with the self, they are particularly useful for writing about trauma. In contrast to many of the approaches we've examined so far, an ekphrastic poem permits a slower entry into the horror.

As both a technique and a rhetorical approach, ekphrastic poetry may already be familiar to many readers. But what can ekphrasis teach us when we reexamine it through the lens of trauma?

I'm struck by how frequently poems about art become an opportunity to meditate on the wounded self. In Book 1 of *The Aeneid*, for example, Aeneas finds himself in Carthage standing before a mural that depicts—from first to last—all the battles of the Trojan War. On the wall before him, he faces the horror. The dead are almost rendered living again. There, in bright pigments, is a visual representation of every trauma Aeneas has just fled. Encountering these losses depicted so exquisitely in paint, Aeneas is able to weep at last, observing that there are tears in things, *sunt lacrimae rerum*.

And then there's W. H. Auden's "Musée des Beaux Arts," which is perhaps the most famous ekphrastic poem of the twentieth century. The text meditates on the work of the great Dutch and Flemish painters of Renaissance, their gift for understanding human suffering how effortlessly most of us turn away from other people's pain. "Musée des Beaux Arts" was written in 1938. Its subject is, ostensibly, an oil painting by Pieter Brueghel the Elder, *Landscape with the Fall of Icarus*. But the poem can also be read as an indictment of the world's indifference to what was happening in Europe in that decade: Germany's march toward invasion, war, and genocide.

Paul Tran's "Landscape with the Fall of Icarus: Oil on Canvas: Pieter Brueghel: 1520" takes up Auden's subject of scrutiny. In Tran's poem, we encounter the same painting. Even some of the language of "Musée des Beaux Arts" finds its way into this twenty-first-century text. But for Tran, the painting is an opportunity to examine an experience of sexual assault and a father's unbearable complicity—his betrayal of his own child.

Whereas Auden uses the oil painting to write about international passivity and political inaction, Tran turns to the work of art as a means of speaking about a very private and intimate violation. They apply the myth of Daedalus and Icarus to their own story of sexual abuse. As a curator in a museum might, the speaker directs our gaze toward a reading of the painting that we might otherwise miss. They caution us that the story of Icarus isn't really a narrative about hubris. Instead, Tran explains, we should recognize how this narrative has eclipsed the tale of a boy who is hurt merely because he follows his father.

Ancient myth is refigured. The painting finds a new form as well. In Brueghel's canvas, Icarus appears as a tiny presence, only his bare legs emerging from the frothy water. The eye barely observes the drowning child. Instead, we focus on the Flemish landscape in its soothing shades of cream, pale green, and brief splashes of red. We notice the puffed sails of the ship. We watch the horse dragging a plough through the pale dirt.

Tran changes this point of view. Now, Icarus's suffering is evident as is the speaker's pain. Their trauma occupies the entire scene, stretching almost to the frame. Ekphrasis is a mode of interpretation. It isn't meant to be an objective restatement of what any viewer might see. Rather, the art object filters through the speaker's trauma, so that some details come to the foreground while others disappear into the distance.

In her poem "The Facts of Art," Natalie Diaz takes as her subject a Hopi basket woven in the early twentieth century. The basket as art object allows Diaz to enter the mesas of Arizona, where she recounts a history of erasure in long lines and cascading stanzas.

The Facts of Art

woven plaque basket with sunflower designs, Hopi,
Arizona, before 1935

from an American Indian basketry exhibit in
Portsmouth, Virginia

The Arizona highway sailed across the desert—
a gray battleship drawing a black wake,
halting at the foot of the orange mesa,
unwilling to go around.

Hopi men and women—brown, and small, and claylike
peered down from their tabletops at yellow tractors, water trucks,
and white men blistered with sun—red as fire ants—towing
sunscreen-slathered wives in glinting Airstream trailers
in caravans behind them.

Elders knew these BIA roads were bad medicine—knew too
that young men listen less and less, and these young Hopi men
needed work, hence set aside their tools, blocks of cottonwood
root
and half-finished Koshari the clown katsinas, then
signed on with the Department of Transportation,

were hired to stab drills deep into the earth's thick red flesh
on First Mesa, drive giant sparking blades across the mesas' faces,
run the drill bits so deep they smoked, bearding all the Hopi men
in white—*Bad Spirits*, said the Elders—

The blades caught fire, burned out—*Ma'Saw is angry*, the Elders said.
New blades were flown in by helicopter. While Elders dreamed
their arms and legs had been cleaved off and their torsos were
flung

over the edge of a dinner table, the young Hopi men went
back to work cutting the land into large chunks of rust.

Nobody noticed at first—not the white workers,
not the Indian workers—but in the mounds of dismantled mesa,
among the clods and piles of sand,
lay the small gray bowls of babies' skulls.

Not until they climbed to the bottom did they see
the silvered bones glinting from the freshly sliced dirt-and-rock
wall—
a mausoleum mosaic, a sick tapestry: the tiny remains
roused from death's dusty cradle, cut in half, cracked,
wrapped in time-tattered scraps of blankets.

Let's call it a day, the white foreman said.
That night, all the Indian workers got sad-drunk—got sick
—while Elders sank to their kivas in prayer. Next morning,
as dawn festered on the horizon, state workers scaled the mesas,
knocked at the doors of pueblos that had them, hollered
into those without them,

demanding the Hopi men come back to work—then begging
them—
then buying them whiskey—begging again—finally sending their
white
wives up the dangerous trail etched into the steep sides
to buy baskets from Hopi wives and grandmothers
as a sign of treaty.

When that didn't work, the state workers called the Indians lazy,
sent their sunhat-wearing wives back up to buy more baskets—
katsinas too—then called the Hopis good-for-nothings,
before begging them back once more.

We'll try again in the morning, the foreman said.
But the Indian workers never returned—
The BIA's and DOT's calls to work went unanswered,
as the fevered Hopis stayed huddled inside.

The small bones half-buried in the crevices of mesa—
in the once-holy darkness of silent earth and always-night—
smiled or sighed beneath the moonlight, while white women
in Airstream trailers wrote letters home

praising their husbands' patience, describing the lazy savages:
such squalor in their stone and plaster homes—cobs of corn stacked
floor to ceiling against crumbling walls—their devilish ceremonies
and the barbaric way they buried their babies,
oh, and those beautiful, beautiful baskets.

As a highway is widened through the desert, something terrible is discovered, what Diaz describes as "the small gray bowls of babies' skulls" and other remains. The Hopi workers are devasted by what has been unearthed and do not return to the job site, while the foreman reads their refusal to work as "lazy." Ultimately, as the Hopi families mourn this encounter with the traumatized past, their new white neighbors learn nothing from the experience.

"The Facts of Art" is a highly narrative poem. In fact, reading the text, it's easy to see the kind of research, archival work, and perhaps gathering of testimony that must have gone into drafting such a piece. Each stanza is vividly rendered: the landscape, the people who inhabit it, their temporary and more permanent homes.

In the poem's final two lines, Diaz captures how the white wives come to fetishize "those beautiful, beautiful baskets" all while speaking with contempt about the Indigenous families living nearby. The white women arrive at an aesthetic appreciation for the exquisitely wrought handicrafts, but their admiration for the baskets is empty; they refuse to see the Hopi artists as people, autonomous human beings entitled to their grief and loss. Thus, as poet Rachel Zucker writes in *The Poetry of Wrongness*, "The basket is an inanimate witness to the systematic oppression and displacement of the Hopi people and the destruction of Hopi art, culture, and lands." In this way, the basket serves as an instigating emblem in the poem—an object that is both an entrance into the story and a resonant figure in itself.

I suspect that poets are attracted to writing about works of art because the task of making a painting can resemble the labor of constructing a poem. Both processes require focus, attention to detail, an awareness and appreciation of artifice. Many ekphrastic poems can be read as metaphors for the poet's own work. A poem about the writing of poetry is known as an *ars poetica*, Latin for "the art of poetry." The ars poetica has an ancient history dating back to Horace and remains a vital practice in twenty-first-century poetics. In many contemporary poetry collections, an ars poetica (disguised as ekphrasis) serves as the book's mission statement. It allows the poet to communicate a collection's values, its narrative and aesthetic goals.

Early on in this book, I tell the story of my mother, who was held prisoner by a violent man when she was a young woman. Because this trauma has had such a profound impact on my own worldview, I have frequently revisited this narrative through poems and essays. In *The Arranged Marriage*, a collection of prose poems, I write about my mother's experience with trauma as well as its aftermath—its consequence not only for her personal and professional life but also its long-lasting impact on her health.

"Eros and Psyche" is an ars poetica hidden inside ekphrasis. The poem makes an argument about what poets have the power to do. Within the text, we can temporarily freeze time. We can keep trauma away.

Eros and Psyche

> From a certain vantage point they could be lovers—the man with his arms encircling my mother, and both of them gone marble. He has woken her with the sound of broken wings. Her blanket is polished rock, cold and weighted to the bed. From this angle the knife is hidden, although it's there, the way an arrow is always shooting through this story, desire a dart that finds the tender spot. Bodies make a space for gods to intervene. Tonight if there are souls like butterflies, then they have stilled. If beauty could be bolted in a box, if a deity could say, Don't open this, then my mother might stay asleep forever, unbothered by the monument of those hands.

The speaker considers Antonio Canova's exquisite sculpture from 1787, "Eros and Psyche," a beautiful depiction of the story from Greek myth. Carved from luminous stone, the piece illustrates the moment in which Cupid finds his beloved unconscious and revives her. After inhaling deadly, poisonous vapors, Psyche has fallen into a permanent sleep. Only Cupid's kiss can wake her.

The poem notes how trauma is only visible from "a certain vantage point." This is one of the problems with trauma. It can remain hidden. It can be objectified, rendered delicate, even lovely. Worst of all, when it comes to some kinds of violence, onlookers may refuse to admit that a woman has been hurt. When my mother reported to the police how the handyman broke into her apartment and kept her hostage for twenty-four hours, how he hit her and held a knife to her throat, she was dismissed as an angry girlfriend. They ignored the bruises on her face and the ligature marks at her wrists. The police officers said my mother should go home. *Just tell him you're sorry and won't do it again*, they advised.

Throughout the poem, the speaker places the image of Psyche and Eros over that of her mother being woken by the stranger. Myth and reality merge into one scene. In writing the piece, Canova's sculpture allowed me to reflect on the complexity of art-making. Both the sculptor and the poet must be dispassionate in their work. They cut away at stone or at language, looking for an ideal form. Occasionally they must pause to stand at a neutral distance and consider the effects of the composition. They must find a pleasing balance between beauty and grief. "Eros and Psyche" ends with a wish that the poem could, in the way of a marble sculpture, fix time so that the mother "might stay asleep forever, unbothered by the monument of those hands." The poem wants to believe that art can do this—that it can protect the mother, ensuring she will never be woken into the sharp blows of trauma.

Writing Your Way In

1. In the manner of Natalie Diaz's "The Facts of Art," write an ekphrastic poem that includes archival or historical research. What facts about trauma are revealed through such research?
2. Write an ekphrastic poem that is also an ars poetica. What does the work of art say about your own efforts to represent trauma through poetry?

CHAPTER 14

Self-Implications

How does the poem become part of the trauma?
For what is the poem to blame?

To implicate is to imply. It is also to show that someone has an intimate connection, usually to a crime. Implications are incriminating. Originally, the word suggested an intertwining or entangling, from the Latin *implicare*.

Many poems that engage with trauma speak from the perspective of the victim or survivor. These texts generally condemn someone else; the speaker's pain has been caused by a perpetrator, a bystander, or a great and malevolent force such as war or climate change. But other poems may be voiced by a witness who is less directly involved. This speaker's duty is to stand back and record, to corroborate, and to acknowledge their own relationship to the hurt. When a poem engages in an act of self-implication, the speaker is enmeshed. The speaker turns a critical gaze on the self. The poem takes a rhetorical position, saying, *Here is my part in all this.*

In her debut collection, *Seam*, Tarfia Faizullah tells the story of the Birangonas, women raped by the Pakistan Army during the Bangladesh liberation war of the 1970s. After the conflict ended, the Birangonas became paradoxical figures, simultaneously named war heroines and viewed as impure. Rather than working solely in an archive or translating previously gathered testimonies into poems,

Faizullah went to Bangladesh and interviewed a number of the Birangonas. These interviews are foundational to *Seam*. But the figure of the Interviewer becomes central to the text as well, so that the reader's attention is called not only to the testimony itself but also to act of collecting and transforming that testimony.

In her poem "The Interviewer Acknowledges Shame," Faizullah essentially breaks the fourth wall, erasing the space between speaker and poet.

The Interviewer Acknowledges Shame

After she has ducked through
 the low-slung metal shack, the war-
raped women she's come
 to visit offer tea drowsy with sweet.
They begin to speak, unlocking
 the desiccated coffins of their grief.
The video camera's lens blinks
 on their dawn-thin faces until daylight
spools itself back into darkness.
 Anything, she says, *you would like*
to tell me, anything you can
 remember. She ducks back under
the clothesline heavy with faded saris
 out to the main road. The rickshawallah
pedals across town to a small,
 heat-spattered hotel room, and after,
she wraps a dark silk scarf around
 herself until twilight. She rubs her eyes
riverbank-raw until she lies
 on the hard narrow bed and begins
to touch herself. After the familiar
 arched shuddering, she wants to cry,
because that, at least, might be

redemption for each broken body
that can't be restored. She doesn't
feel shame's dark-circled tightening
after waking fully-clothed
to the mirror, dust-webbed, nor
when she boards the bus back
to the city. Sunlight fades to the open
windows into white dreams.
A child bends down to elevate
a pink blossom away
from a green field. It's when she returns
to a borrowed flat, begins
to strip off her travel-pungent clothes
and smells her own body's resinous
musk. It's when she sits naked
at the desk to rewind & fast-forward
through all the pixelated footage
of the women's kerosened lives.
It's when she begins to write
about it in third person, as though
it was that simple
to unnail myself from my own body.

Notice how in the final four lines of the poem, Faizullah shifts abruptly from third person into first person. "[T]o unnail myself from my own body," the poem ends. It's a moment of self-implication in which the poet-speaker acknowledges that she is using the women's testimonies to create a poem. She's pulling herself away from herself—as if she were a nail yanked out of a wooden board—to create a false sense of authorial distance, so that she will not have to confront the risks of her work. But the process isn't "that simple," the poem admits. The speaker can neither divide herself from her own body nor can she fully escape the discomfort of having turned the Birangonas' grief into "desiccated coffins." To make art of other people's trauma is indeed a fraught undertaking.

Poet Paisley Rekdal explores such matters in her book *Appropriate: A Provocation*, where she attempts to define, analyze, and provide guidance for the appropriative work that is so often a part of engaging with experiences beyond our own:

> When it comes to writing about or through the lives of others, we have to begin with the desire to respect each other's dignity and difference from ourselves, and this requires an understanding of the history of the individuals we wish to represent. And we also have to begin with the understanding of empathy's limits: we are not all of the same, though we share profound similarities, and certainly feel the same emotions.

Certainly, "The Interviewer Acknowledges Shame" approaches the Birangonas with great respect for the women's dignity as well as an understanding of their history. I would also suggest it's Faizullah's self-awareness and attentiveness to the ethics of crafting poems that makes *Seam* such a powerful depiction of the effects of rape as a genocidal policy.

Even when a poem's subject matter is extreme pain, writing poetry can be a pleasurable act. "The Interviewer Acknowledges Shame"—with its sensual images, its erotic closing scene—addresses this problem. Faizullah's poem argues it's not masturbation that causes the speaker to feel ashamed; it's the act of aestheticizing atrocity that's disgraceful. It's the moment when the poet-speaker "begins to write" about interviewing the Birangona "in third person" that merits shame. This rhetorical move is crucial to the effectiveness of the poem and to *Seam* as a whole. Because the speaker consistently shows that she understands her position in relation to the trauma and, for that matter, that she recognizes how her poems are appropriating the traumas of the Birangonas, the book is both a source of testimony as well as a treatise on what it means to turn testimony into poetry: the difficulties, the pitfalls, the thorny ethics of this undertaking.

Ilya Kaminsky's much-anthologized "We Lived Happily During the War" shares with Faizullah's poem an interest in point of view. Kaminsky too sees grammar as a strategy for addressing culpability. In the poem, Kaminsky employs the first-person plural "we"; the speaker is part of a larger group—Americans—all of whom share responsibility for a war happening elsewhere in the world:

We Lived Happily During the War

And when they bombed other people's houses, we

protested
but not enough, we opposed them but not

enough. I was
in my bed, around my bed America

was falling: invisible house by invisible house by invisible house.

I took a chair outside and watched the sun.

In the sixth month
of a disastrous reign in the house of money

in the street of money in the city of money in the country of money,
our great country of money, we (forgive us)

lived happily during the war.

In an interview about his poem—which went viral on social media following Russia's invasion of Ukraine in 2022—Kaminsky explains that "We Lived Happily During the War" explores "the happiness of living with our backs turned—ignorant bliss." The text moves from well-intentioned gestures to an admission that these small actions are insufficient: "we / protested / but not enough, we opposed them but not / enough." In the first half of the piece, the poet's radical enjambments create a jarring effect as we swing back and forth between halfhearted activism and the recognition that bourgeois political engagement rarely makes a difference (and is, quite frequently, little more than self-aggrandizement).

Kaminsky characterizes the poem as "heavy with irony about the greatness of our capitalist nation." The speaker acknowledges, quite willingly, that life in "our great country of money" insulates us for other people's trauma. Money is a delicious featherbed that cushions and soothes. Money is a pair of earplugs that blocks sharp sounds. If there is war, it happens somewhere across a wide ocean. If bombs are falling, they're landing on houses far away from here.

"We Lived Happily During the War" works because it implicates the speaker and all the rest of us with cool, sly detachment. Only that parenthetical "forgive us"—like a brief prayer of atonement—reveals that the speaker feels a greater shame than is initially apparent. One day, the poem implies, we will have to reckon with the consequences of our inaction. And we will need to beg for forgiveness.

Writing Your Way In

1. Write a poem that—in the way of Tarfia Faizullah's "The Interviewer Acknowledges Shame"—examines your position in relation to someone else's trauma.
2. Emulating Ilya Kaminsky's approach, write a draft in first-person plural. Use the "we" to explore the passivity of bystanders in the face of trauma.

CHAPTER 15

Questions

Why do we ask? What do we hope from our asking?
Who will answer us?

In the Bible, when Job is tormented with a litany of losses—his home, his children, his good health, everything that made life lovely now swept away—the character calls out to God. Job asks why he has been given so much suffering. And, confronted with the agony of a man, God's answer is to descend as a whirlwind, a rage of rhetorical questions. *Where were you?* God demands. *Have you done the things that I've done?* The questions drag on for many pages, a coiling storm of words, while Job trembles with terror.

Some people ask questions to learn. Some to brush away confusion. Some to humble themselves. Like God in the Book of Job, there are those who ask questions to prove their own rightness. Others to express their confusion in the world. They ask questions because they're searching for dialogue. Their questions are like reaching for another person's hand.

In Fady Joudah's "Mimesis," the poet presents a tiny scene in which a father and daughter consider evicting a spider from its web, which is woven between the handles of the little girl's bicycle. Their discussion about the arachnid leads the daughter to ask a question. And the question, in turn, becomes an opportunity for the poet to consider displacement and exile.

Mimesis

My daughter
                    wouldn't hurt a spider
That had nested
Between her bicycle handles
For two weeks
She waited
Until it left of its own accord

If you tear down the web I said
It will simply know
This isn't a place to call home
And you'd get to go biking

She said that's how others
Become refugees isn't it?

Fady Joudah, a physician and the son of two refugees, frequently explores the Nakba, the catastrophic displacement of Palestinians from their homes and their land during the 1948 Arab-Israeli war. In "Mimesis," a brief conversation between a father and daughter stands in for a deeply traumatic historic event, one which continues to have disastrous, geopolitical consequences for Palestinians.

Without its closing question, "Mimesis" would remain a small, domestic moment. The father suggests to his child that she simply remove the web, so that she can "get to go biking." All he sees is that his daughter needs help solving a problem. He wants her to have fun, perhaps, even to stop worrying about something as trivial as a spider.

The young girl who functions as the moral center of the text. Rather than viewing the spider as an inconvenience, she recognizes it is a life worthy of dignity and respect. Hearing her father's advice, she asks a question: "that's how others / Become refugees isn't it?"

The poem ends there. We don't know how the father might have responded, if given a chance. But a reader is likely to feel rebuked, a little ashamed not to have seen the arachnid as the daughter does, not to have recognized the web as a home, the tearing down of the gossamer an act of violence. Like a religious parable, Joudah's poem is didactic. It offers a lesson through the innocent voice of a child who asks a simple question of her father.

Mimesis means "mimicry" or "imitation." In literature, it is the idea that a piece of artistic writing can function like a mirror, representing both our external realities and the interiority of our thoughts and feelings. In Joudah's poem, the spider cast out of its precarious web is mimetic of the story of refugees dislodged from their homes. For poets who speak as exiles, posing questions can be a way of feeling toward a landscape of safety and belonging. Displaced not only from landscape but also from culture and language, these poets use the interrogatory to express the inherent unease, grief, and confusion of the exilic state.

Of course, not every question is posed with sincerity. Rebecca Hazelton's "Questions About the Wife" uses the interrogative mood to call attention to the traumas of a confining, abusive relationship.

Questions About the Wife

I'm having trouble understanding the wife.
The wife seems like she is only there as a foil to your actions.
I want to know how the wife feels when you drag her
and your son down into the basement to start a new religion.
The religion has something to do with cowering
before a force greater than yourself and then being buried alive.
I want to know how the wife behaves in small, enclosed spaces:
if she is trying to comfort your son by telling him Daddy likes
to play funny games, or if she is already visualizing
herself walking into a women's shelter, your son
on her back and maybe, because this is a fantasy,

she carries a burning torch, like an angry villager, or a goddess.
Does the wife merit any revenge after you weed whack
the coffee table? Does she agree with you that the coffee table
is yours to destroy because you built it? What has she built
in the house that is hers to destroy? What kind of childhood
has the wife endured that allows her to understand you?
In her past life or lives, was the wife ever a shepherdess?
Does she see you as a sort of Pan, goatish, and pricked
by ticks, but also very well-endowed? When the wife transforms
into a tree can she still think or is she just a green haze
inside, an idea of growing? I would like to see the wife
peel off that bark, leaving only enough for modesty's sake,
although as this is your poem, we can take a bit more off.
I want to see her uproot herself, pick up the house and shake it.
How many people fall out?
The wife has something about her the Germans
would call *unheimlich*. I sometimes catch a glimpse of the wife
out of the corner of my eye but then I look away.
I cannot look directly at the wife. The wife is a conflagration
of everything dear. I wonder sometimes if she is faking;
There is a certain note she holds too long
so the orgasm is more operatic, less genuine.
When she cries, *Oh my God*, really, she should stutter.
Let's say the wife wakes up in the morning.
You have already made breakfast. Does your kindness feel oppressive?
Does she want to take your weed whacker through the house?
Has she ever, in a fit of anger, destroyed your pornography?
When you found a picture of the wife online with a foreign hand-
print
smacked red on her ass, how quickly did your shock turn to arousal?
Are you aware the wife is breaking down in public places,
and sometimes cannot move for thirty minutes? Sometimes
her arm goes entirely numb from the shoulder down. I think the
wife

might need some fine-tuning, some elbow grease,
some wrenching apart, and then reassembling.

There are generally three ways that a "you" can operate in a poem. First, the speaker might address another character in the text. Alternatively, the speaker can address the reader of the poem; she talks to us, as our eyes move across the words she is saying. Finally, the speaker can address the self, using second person to establish emotional distance.

"Questions About the Wife" appears to use the first of these three approaches. The speaker, who is a kind of literary figure herself, is communicating with another character in the piece. Initially, the whole poem reads like a humorous monologue that a woman might deliver in a creative writing workshop. Her questions appear to be a scathing critique of a male classmate who doesn't seem to know how to construct complex female characters.

But it very quickly becomes apparent that the speaker is, in fact, the wife. The details are too intimate and precise not to be her own experiences. "Are you aware the wife is breaking down in public places," the speaker asks, "and sometimes cannot move for thirty minutes? Sometimes / her arm goes entirely numb from the shoulder down." It's also clear that her interlocutor is the husband: violent, volatile, tyrannical. And, given that this man is so unstable, can we blame the speaker for reframing the conversation so that it seems to occur within the (somewhat) safe space of a classroom? The speaker can pretend that she's only responding to a draft of story, when in fact she's confessing her own traumas and presenting a devastating portrait of a very broken marriage.

Both "Mimesis" and "Questions About the Wife" argue that trauma is unanswerable. The poems don't even try to provide rejoinders. They choose to end with uncertainty, their questions allowed to float unanswered and unresolved in the white space that follows.

Writing Your Way In

1. Write a list poem that contains a series of furious, traumatized questions. Direct these questions toward an entity with significant power, such as a government or a deity. In the way of Job, demand answers. Do not allow the poem to offer resolution.
2. As Fady Joudah does in "Mimesis," write a poem that ends with a question that is innocent and sincere. Allow the question to circle around some important truth about trauma.
3. Imitating Rebecca Hazelton's "Questions About the Wife," write a poem in which the speaker is asking pointed questions of another character in the text. Use humor to disguise or deflect the trauma that exists between these two people.

CHAPTER 16

Unlikables

What do we do with the unpleasant voices of our pain?

When I first began to read the literature of the Shoah, I was surprised by how often survivors are depicted as repulsive, ruined human beings. While I understood the brutal wounds that trauma leaves, it nonetheless struck me as subversive to show survivors in such an unappealing light. In *Maus*, Vladek Spiegelman is stingy and racist. In *Rosa*, Cynthia Ozick's title character is embittered and cynical. The poems of Paul Celan often speak in a relentless, evasive voice, one that doesn't care how easily it is understood. Through their unlikable characters and speakers, these texts argue that trauma doesn't make us better or kinder. In most cases, trauma leaves us little more than broken. The fractures of trauma are ugly. They are rough-edged and resist mending.

It's fitting—given that so many writers who explore the Shoah are Jewish—that there should be a rejection of redemptive storytelling in Holocaust prose and poetry. The belief that there might be redemption through suffering is not a Jewish concept. Much of Holocaust literature resists Christlike readings of pain, refusing the consolation that such agony might lead to salvation.

In an interview, historian Dominick LaCapra criticizes redemptive narratives. He says:

> If you believe in the Biblical story, you do, in a sense, believe in a grand narrative of history, so that everything, even the most disastrous catastrophes, will ultimately make sense to you—maybe not now, but at some point of illumination in the future. This no longer seems to be feasible to many—or at least a significant number of—people.

LaCapra is talking about representations of the Shoah. But his point could as easily be applied to any story of trauma. Confronted with extreme pain, we have the impulse to construct what he calls a "grand narrative." We want to mold an agonized story into a reassuring form that says, *Something valuable came out of this.* It's hard not to shape the trauma so that it resolves in the consolation of meaning:

> If you take the conventional narrative structure itself—with a beginning, a middle and an end, whereby the end recapitulates the beginning after the trials of the middle, and gives you (at least on the level of insight), some realization of what it was all about—there's a sense in which the conventional narrative is redemptive.

This is a difficult urge to fight when constructing art that engages with trauma. And we may feel the same inclination toward the redemptive when constructing an individual speaker in a poem. It's tempting to show every victim or survivor as virtuous. Haven't they gone through enough already? Why should we articulate the ugliness of trauma, how often it leaves people self-absorbed, difficult to know, or even hard to love? But if we write the traumatized speakers of our poems as wholly gracious figures, we'll end up with disingenuous art.

This work is especially challenging when we're writing about our own traumas. When we're in pain, we want empathy, to have readers see us as sympathetic, perhaps even heroic. We want the speakers of our poems to be admired for what they have endured. I would argue, however, that in a complex portrait of trauma we should make room for the unlikable parts of ourselves.

Katie Farris explores the ugliness of trauma in *Standing in the Forest of Being Alive*, a collection of poems that recount a terrible cancer diagnosis and the grueling treatments that follow. The traumas here are both physical and emotional. They are so awful that the speaker responds alternatingly with fury, humor, and even surprising moments of sexual desire. "Tell It Slant," one of the opening poems in the book, recounts the moment in which the speaker first receives her diagnosis.

Tell It Slant

You float in the MRI gloam,
several spiculated masses;
I name you "cactus,"
carcinoma be damned—you make
a desert of all
of me.

Have I said it slant enough?
Here's a shot between
the eyes: Six days before
my thirty-seventh birthday,
a stranger called and said,
You have cancer. Unfortunately.
And then hung up the phone.

The speaker is furious in this poem, and with good reason. She resents being pressured to tell the truth "slant"—as Emily Dickinson advises—through figurative language. In the first stanza, she gives in to this pressure, naming her carcinoma a "cactus." She calls the MRI a "gloam," that time just after sunset when there's still a faint presence of light in the sky. And the speaker herself says she is transformed by the cancer into a "desert."

In the second stanza, it's no longer the cancer that the speaker seems to address but Emily Dickinson herself. "Have I said it slant enough?" the speaker demands of the nineteenth-century poet, enraged by Dickinson's didacticism. From there on, Farris rejects slanted, oblique approaches. "Here's a shot between / the eyes," she says. It's the last example of figurative language in the poem. The facts, as she relays them, are swift and direct as medicine delivered through a port. The rest of the poem is spoken without any obliquity. We're told when the speaker received the news (on her thirty-seventh birthday), how (over the phone), and by whom (a stranger). Worst of all, we're given the exact, blunt words. That adverb, "*Unfortunately*," is unbearably understated and devoid of empathy.

The speaker isn't likable. Nor should she be. She's enraged: equally disgusted with the caller who delivered the bad news as she is with the cancer. She resents the expectations of poetry, that she is supposed to convert a shattering diagnosis into something lyrical. Here, Dickinson is a stand-in; she symbolizes poetry, representing the unfair demands of the artform.

What I admire about Farris's poem is the speaker's unwillingness to exalt herself. She's not interested in ingratiation. She doesn't need our admiration.

Sandra Beasley takes a different tack in crafting an unlikable speaker. In "Cherry Tomatoes," the poet transforms an ordinary food into an emblem for coming-of-age in an extremely broken, unhappy family.

Cherry Tomatoes

Little bastards of vine.
Little demons by the pint.
Red eggs that never hatch,
just collapse and rot. When

my mom told me to gather
their grubby bodies

into my skirt, I'd cry. You
and your father, she'd chide—

the way, each time I kicked
and wailed against sailing,
my dad shook his head, said
You and your mother.

Now, a city girl, I ease one
loose from its siblings,
from its clear plastic coffin,
place it on my tongue.

Just to try. The smooth
surface resists, resists,
and erupts in my mouth:
seeds, juice, acid, blood

of a perfect household.
The way, when I finally
went sailing, my stomach
was rocked from inside

out. Little boat, big sea.
Handful of skinned sunsets.

The child becomes a stand-in for each parent's fury with their spouse. "You / and your father," says the mother to the daughter. "You and your mother," the father observes, shaking his head in exasperation. It's a household gone bad as an old cherry tomato, seemingly "perfect" on the outside but unbearably sour within. The speaker finds herself trapped between these two rigid adults, who view her as the personification of everything that is wrong with the other parent, their home coffinlike, a plastic container full of sad, rotten fruit.

Hurt people hurt people, as the saying goes. And certainly, the speaker in the poem seems wounded. Her voice is brittle, sharp, at times hyperbolic in expressing how she has been damaged by her parents' domestic warfare. It's easy to guess what she has learned about kindness and how difficult it will be for her to love others in turn. But Beasley's speaker is also engaging; she's funny and playful, skilled at turning these critical, angry people into intriguing characters. Each time I read "Cherry Tomatoes," I'm discomfited by my reaction to the text. I appreciate the poem's cleverness, its gift of metaphor, its way with images. I'm the unlikable one: charmed by the droll turns of phrase, losing sight of the piece's engagement with trauma, the argument that trauma remains trauma even when it can prepare nice dinners or steer an elegant sailboat along the Potomac.

These poems resist the comforting notion that trauma ennobles us. No, they say, suffering does not redeem us. Their task is not to reassure readers but to depict pain accurately, showing us a wound that may be unpleasant or disturbing to encounter.

Writing Your Way In

1. Incorporate elements of a Biblical story, telling a "grand narrative" of the trauma you wish to explore. Do not end the poem with a redemptive gesture. Allow the suffering to exist without meaning.
2. Write a draft in which the speaker presents trauma lyrically then proceeds to undo that lyricism, speaking about the hurt in frank, direct terms. The poem can express anger, even rage.
3. What do you believe poems of trauma are burdened with saying or doing? "Tell It Slant" pushes back against Dickinson's famous dictum about how to tell the truth. Write a draft that rejects what you see as an unfair expectation of poetry.
4. Write a poem that transforms an ordinary food into a symbol of the trauma you wish to explore.

CHAPTER 17

Comedies

Why do we joke about pain? Where do we find the humor?

Patricia Lockwood's "Rape Joke" seemed like it was everywhere in 2013. The text was shared breathlessly across social-media platforms, discussed, parsed, debated online, analyzed both by appreciative critics and shocked readers. It was the verse equivalent of laughing at a funeral. It was gallows humor given poetic form.

Explaining the dialogue that led to "Rape Joke," poet and essayist Elisa Gabbert writes,

> I associate it with the discourse surrounding an incident at a comedy club in 2012, when a woman in the audience yelled, "Actually, rape jokes are never funny!" at the comedian onstage, who then reportedly said, "Wouldn't it be funny if that girl got raped by like, five guys right now?" It's shocking, and yet unsurprising, that the comic defended this threatening, utterly unfunny remark as a joke.

There is, of course, the taboo of a comedian cracking jokes about sexual assault. And then there's "Rape Joke," which breaks an even greater taboo. A woman takes the microphone from a man—a gesture not without danger—so that he is forced into silence while she speaks.

The poem asks if rape jokes can ever be funny. It's a piece that tries to make sense of how we speak and write about sexual assault. How do we parse its horrors and absurdities, its grim ironies? And where in the story of a rape might the joke reside? Is the humor found in the rapist's ridiculous facial hair? In the speaker's parents when they learn of the assault and don't know how to react? Or maybe the humor is embodied by the speaker herself, her refusal to engage in self-pity, her unwillingness to let the rapist have the final say.

Gabbert concludes,

> The right to tell a "rape joke" belongs to the victim—and there's subversive power in using the formal properties of the joke to complicate, rather than trivialize, trauma. Humor can be used as a defense mechanism . . . but it's also a reclamation of control—a refusal to be told how to feel about your own lived (and relived) experience.

Lockwood's poem is audacious because it seizes the microphone. She pushes the comic offstage. Transgressive and defiant, the poem stands in the spotlight, delivering a long monologue that no one can interrupt.

"Rape Joke" engages obliquely with the relationship between trauma and theatricality. Jason Schneiderman's "Dramaturgy" examines the intersection of pain and performance more directly. In the poem, a playwright describes the experience of writing a stage play about the Shoah. While the subject of genocide couldn't be more serious, the speaker's voice—self-important, a bit grandiose—is essential to the poem's comedy. Those of us who spend our lives in the literary arts are likely to have encountered these sorts of characters: writers who are sincerely committed to their work but who are also distressingly, comically misguided. Schneiderman occupies this persona flawlessly. He gives a perfect performance of the earnest writer who is unable to recognize his own play as schlock.

Dramaturgy

I'm writing a play about a Kommandant at Auschwitz
who recognizes one of the Jewish prisoners
as a famous poet, and as the Kommandant
has poetic aspirations himself, he pulls the prisoner
away from the work detail to receive poetry lessons
from the celebrated Jewish writer. The bulk of the play
is their discussions of poetry, which the poet
is initially reluctant to have, the power differential
being so stark, and though he flatters the Kommandant
at first, when he begins to see his Nazi pupil's
true devotion to the art, as well as his untrained
and untapped talent, he goes to work in earnest,
and at times they are both simply lovers
of the German language, though the truth of their
situation often interrupts. In the last act,
the Kommandant is on trial for his crimes,
and in the days before he is to be executed,
he begs the poets to publish his work under his own name—
the Nazi's writing under the Jew's name—
because as a Nazi, he feels his own name is disgraced,
but he believes so strongly in poetry that it matters
more to him that his work survive than that anyone
know it was his work. The play is pulled entirely
from my imagination, a careful rereading
of Simon Wiesenthal's *The Sunflower*, and the poetic ideas
of Rilke and Goethe, with a smattering of Nietzsche.
In readings of the play, the Kommandant
has seemed more noble than I had intended—in many ways,
more noble than the Jew, because the Jew is suffering
by no fault of his own, while the Kommandant is tortured
by conscience, and driven by a sense of poetic calling

that separates him from the Germans around him.
On the morning of the third workshop reading, I watched
a video of two Russians on an ice-dancing reality show
performing as Jews in Auschwitz. I was sickened,
even though I couldn't follow the pantomimed action,
and I wondered if I was producing Holocaust kitsch myself,
if my work was as disgusting as theirs, though I knew
if I asked any of my team, they would reassure me
that I am doing important work that rises to the level
of art. Last night, during a break in the workshop of the play,
I told the story of how my grandmother, upon learning
that her entire family had died in the camps,
had burned the photo albums of everyone she had loved.
I have told that story many, many times,
without feeling much more than regret, or sympathy,
but this time I broke down crying, and I couldn't stop.
Everyone at the table came to comfort me,
and I felt ridiculous, but the only thing I could say was,
"It's time for us to go. This isn't a place we can live anymore."
I left the studio embarrassed, and later that day,
I resigned from the production. I don't think they believed
that I was serious, and they'll expect me to show up
at the next table reading. I won't. The play will go on
though I can have nothing more to do with it.
This morning, after taking a shirt off the hanger,
I looked in the mirror and realized I hadn't put it on.
Without thinking, I had started packing a bag.

When the speaker describes the play as "a careful rereading / of Simon Wiesenthal's *The Sunflower*, and the poetic ideas / of Rilke and Goethe, with a smattering of Nietzsche," we should understand that this imagined piece of theater engages with the Shoah in the most predictable ways, asking only the most banal questions about the relationship between poetry and salvation. The more the speaker describes this play, the likelier it seems that he is in the process of ushering a very bad work of art onto the stage.

But then the poem takes a turn. The speaker watches "two Russians on an ice-dancing reality show / performing as Jews in Auschwitz." Disgusted by what he sees on the TV screen, he realizes that he might be "producing Holocaust kitsch" himself. Awakened from the making of bad art, the speaker spends the rest of the poem coming to the recognition that the pressing matter is not the clichéd story of the Kommandant and the imprisoned Jewish poet. Rather, he suddenly feels his own ancestral trauma intersecting with the current moment, one in which Jews continue to experience antisemitism and the resulting feelings of dislocation. During a table read of the play, the speaker begins to weep, telling the room, "It's time for us to go. This isn't a place we can live anymore." The speaker's breakdown prepares us for the final lines of the poem in which he realizes that "Without thinking" he has "started packing a bag." In many Jewish families, there remains the belief that we should always keep a bag packed. We must always be ready to flee, the possibility of violence imminent as a knock on the door.

There's the old saw that comedy is tragedy plus time. I like the ambiguity of this adage. On the one hand, it suggests that good timing is the key to comedy. But it also implies that, if given enough time, we can find the comedic even in the tragic. Both "Rape Joke" and "Dramaturgy" have impeccable timing. They also use the effects of time to establish distance from their respective traumas, arguing that comedy and tragedy are not mutually exclusive. "Rape Joke"—with its dry, keenly observed details—is built on the act of retrospection. The poem recollects vividly not only the assault itself but also the aftermath of the rape. "Dramaturgy" takes readers through the speaker's perception of art and its relationship to trauma in real time. We are allowed to see the exact moment in which the speaker's mind shifts and he begins to question whether his own work is "disgusting."

Comedy doesn't erase tragedy. It doesn't obscure the pain. Humor is like a piece of gauze, a scrim the poet hangs in front of the glare of trauma; it's a cloth that diffuses the piercing light.

Writing Your Way In

1. Write a poem that catalogs all the possible jokes one could make about the trauma you wish to explore. Set the narrative in the distant past. Commit to finding the farces, absurdities, and paradoxes of this trauma. Write specific and exact images, sensory details that speak to the trauma's immediacy.
2. Write a piece that emulates "Dramaturgy." Your speaker should be too serious and sincere (comically so). In the final third of the draft, allow the speaker to have a realization, to experience a dramatic shift in perspective. After this turn, the speaker can no longer understand the trauma in the same way and is transformed by this new, disturbing knowledge.

CHAPTER 18

Joys

How does joy live adjacent to trauma?
Why should we acknowledge the resilience of delight?

Not long ago, I wrote a book about our sense of taste. Researching my subject, I learned that salt magnifies other flavors. The sour dill pickle needs salt to be most fully itself. We stir salt into cake batter to elicit both the bitter and sweet of the chocolate. I wrote about sweat—that it is proof of the body's continuing efforts to live. I wrote about tears. Crying is a necessary act of cleansing the eye as well as evidence that grief need not turn us to pillars of salt. The metaphor is easy to reach from here: tears make the joys more vibrant. The taste of delight is intensified by a dash of grief.

Near the end of "Rewindings and Restorations," I write, "we can insist that our poems become sites of fleeting grace. We can assert the right to joy. In the brief space of the poem, we can unravel or push out the trauma. We can allow, however temporarily, the possibility of defiant, life-affirming alternatives to the pain." In his collection of essays, *Inciting Joy*, poet and nonfiction writer Ross Gay poses a series of questions about the emotion:

> What happens if joy is not separate from pain? What if joy and pain are fundamentally tangled up with one another? Or even more to the point, what if joy is not entangled with pain, or suf-

> fering, or sorrow, but is also what emerges from how we care for each other *through* those things? What if joy, instead of refuge or relief from heartbreak, is what effloresces from us as we help each other carry our heartbreaks?

These rhetorical questions are answered in Nomi Stone's "Waiting for Happiness," a text in which joy entangles with sadness, the two emotions equally present in the scene.

Waiting for Happiness

Dog knows when friend will come home
because each hour friend's smell pales,
air paring down the good smell
with its little diamond. It means I miss you
O I miss you, how hard it is to wait
for my happiness, and how good when
it arrives. Here we are in our bodies,
ripe as avocados, softer, brightening
with latencies like a hot, blue core
of electricity: our ankles knotted to our
calves by a thread, womb sparking
with watermelon seeds we swallowed
as children, the heart again badly hurt, trying
and failing. But it is almost five says
the dog. It is almost five.

Stone's poem, as the title announces, is about anticipation. In other words, it's about the moment before happiness arrives. But the poet does not erase trauma altogether. Instead, the text names loss, through the dog's deep longing for its "friend." The canine embodies now-ness, the ability to be present in the present tense. But because the dog is also a creature of the moment, the absence of its dear friend feels all the more difficult to bear.

The joys in Stone's poem are possible because she acknowledges the presence of pain. "The heart" is "again badly hurt, trying / and failing." She doesn't specify what trauma has occurred, but it appears to be of the domestic variety; the poem's references to ripeness, the womb, and seeds points toward difficulties with fertility, perhaps an ongoing failure to conceive and a desire for a child.

Fortunately, the delay of the dog's joy will be very brief, and this fact is itself a source of comfort. "It is almost five," says the poem. We know that soon the friend will arrive—possibly as soon as the poem ends—and the dog will leap into the air, barking with delight, its temporary grief now brushed aside with the wag of an ecstatic tail.

Angela Narciso Torres's beautiful "Fennel" entangles joy with the trauma of losing a parent. The scent of fresh-picked fennel allows the speaker to approach a delicate memory of her mother.

Fennel

It's the season of wild fennel,
perfuming the walking trail with puffs
of licorice. It smells like a candy shop.
The path is dry and caked except
in dips where water pools. Here
and there, feathered fronds wave
hello! hello! like the women brisk
walking on their lunch break. *Fennel!*
fennel! they cheer, wielding their green
pompom bouquets. One of them
hands me a bunch, says they're great
in salads. *Smells delicious*, she adds,
like black licorice! At home, I place them
in water and remember my mother
who loved the chewy treat. And when
she took one from her purse, that scent—
earthy, sharp, wild, sudden, sweet.

After someone dies, it often feels dangerous to remember that person, particularly if the death was traumatic; memory can resemble a dark trail on which it is easy to lose oneself. "Fennel" is indeed a walking poem, but the hike leads us toward deliciousness, not pain. The speaker is on a path perfumed with "puffs / of licorice," the aroma of fresh-cut fennel. She encounters a group of women, full of life and "brisk / walking on their lunch break." They hold bundles of fennel like "pompon bouquets," as if they are cheerleaders for the aromatic and fleeting delights of being alive.

Of all the five senses, smell is most closely linked to memory and to emotion. We process fragrance through the amygdala, almond-shaped clusters of neurons in the brain. Receiving one of these bouquets as a gift, the speaker finally thinks of her mother, "who loved the chewy treat." It is the fennel's fragrance that allows her to venture into the unpredictable forest of memory. She recalls how her mother would pull a fennel bulb "from her purse." The poem ends with a description of the fennel's odor. There's no bleakness here. The reminiscence doesn't trap the reader inside trauma. Instead, the air fills with a scent that seems to express something about who the mother was, her energy, her intensity, and her surprising sweetness.

Writing Your Way In

1. Write a draft that imitates Nomi Stone's "Waiting for Happiness." Allow the character/s in the poem to experience joy tinged with the anticipation of a greater happiness. What is the obstacle? What impedes the character/s from fully experiencing joy?
2. Write a poem in which the taste or scent of a food allows the speaker to experience the mingling of trauma and happiness. Think of this as another exercise in ekphrasis. Begin with the vivid, sensory descriptions before turning inward.

CHAPTER 19

Fixed Forms

Can trauma find a formal paradigm?
What safety in pentameter and rhyme?

So often when speaking about trauma, poets will quote Emily Dickinson's "After great pain, a formal feeling comes—." Dickinson's poem describes the rigidity that we experience following a severe hurt. We become frozen, our bodies machinelike and stiffened, after which there is nothing else to do but to let go, either by succumbing to death or by allowing the ache to recede into the distance of memory.

Of course, poets also admire Dickinson's claim because it allows us to argue that there's a link between pain and certain formal approaches to writing about trauma.

And it's true: poems known as fixed forms can function as safe containers in which to hold devastating subject matter. These poetic structures come with strict rules. They may have a predetermined number of lines. Perhaps they require recurring words or phrases. Many fixed forms are centuries old, having filtered down or having been appropriated into English from other literary traditions, cultures, and languages.

Sometimes the play of fixed form is what we need to write the horror. The challenge of a fixed form can function as a distraction. We busy ourselves with the technical difficulties of writing in rhyme and meter. We concentrate on crafting effective refrains. And by focusing on the restrictions of a form, we can say things that might otherwise be too terrifying to articulate.

Writing in a fixed form also makes an argument about trauma itself. For instance, when we fit a wounded narrative into the narrow space of a sonnet's fourteen lines, we are insisting that it's possible to enclose or surround the pain, albeit briefly. More than that, we're asserting that visible artifice isn't incompatible with our unruliest emotions. We can write in a form that dates to the thirteenth century while still speaking about the terror of *right now*. Analyzing this "highly focused form," poet Phillis Levin writes that

> the sonnet attracts contradictory artistic impulses: in choosing and succumbing to the form, the poet agrees to follow the rules of the sonnet, but that willing surrender releases creative energy. . . . The poet experiences the illusion of control and the illusion of freedom, and from the meeting of those illusions creates the reality of the poem.

Rhina Espaillat's "Suppose," which I discuss in chapter 10, "Counterfactual Histories and Alternate Universes," is a very strict example of an Elizabethan sonnet. Aaron Smith's "Sissy" presents a looser interpretation of the form. The poem veers away from iambic pentameter toward lines of free verse. Throughout the piece, Smith rhymes the word *sissy* with *sissy*, every line ending with the same word. In other words, Smith preserves the spirit of the sonnet while subverting certain expectations that readers might bring to the form. We might say that the poet is queering the sonnet; he pushes against the conventions of meter and rhyme even as he insists that there is plenty of room within this poetic tradition to explore twenty-first-century questions about masculinity.

Sissy

I can't remember my dad calling me a sissy,
but he definitely told me not to be a sissy.
I secretly (or not so secretly) liked all the sissy
things. We had a hunting dog named Sissy.
Really: Sissy. My father nicknamed my sister: Sissy.
Still, he says, "How's Sissy?" and calls her Sissy
when she goes home to visit him. Belinda (Sissy)
is one of the toughest people I know. My sissy
(sister) has kicked someone's ass, which isn't sissy-
ish, I guess, though I want to redefine sissy
into something fabulous, tough, tender, "sissy-
tough." Drag queens are damn tough and sissies.
I'm pretty fucking tough and a big, big sissy,
too. And kind. Tough and kind and happy: a sissy.

The word *sissy* is derogatory. Generally directed at boys and men who are viewed as too fragile, too interested in the softness of women's pursuits, *sissy* is linked etymologically to the word "sister." Smith investigates these roots in the poem. He shows that there's nothing wrong with being seen as effeminate, especially when such femininity is linked to a "fabulous, tough, tender" sister or an equally strong drag queen.

Slurs are intended to silence. Name-calling uses speech to demean, to humiliate, or to smear a person as if with mud. Rather than giving into intimidation, the speaker turns *sissy* into a mark of strength and self-realization. Just as activists once transformed the pink triangle from a symbol of Nazi hatred into an emblem of pride, so does Smith now alter the meaning of *sissy*. He pulls the sting from the word. In removing the trauma that we associate with a verbal attack, Smith reshapes *sissy* into a name that is synonymous with kindness and happiness.

In Natasha Trethewey's "Incident," the poet works in a Malayan form known as the *pantoum* to recall a cross burning that the speaker witnessed as a small child. Pantoums are comprised of quatrains and involve a complex repetition of lines. The second and fourth lines of one stanza become the first and third lines of the succeeding stanza. This pattern can be repeated for as long as the poet wishes; the form doesn't have a predetermined length (although pantoums are most effective if they run at least four stanzas). Importantly, a pantoum closes by returning to its start. The first and third lines of the opening stanza become the second and final lines of the last stanza. This creates a circular effect, as if the poem were a snake devouring its own tail.

Interlocking, doubling back, and constantly returning to earlier moments of narrative, the pantoum is ideally suited to exploring unresolved traumas. In this way, it's possible to see a pantoum as mimetic of the traumatized mind. The form retraces its steps and revisits its anxieties much in the way of certain techniques discussed earlier in this book, such as the fugue state (chapter 4) or the catalog (chapter 1). The pantoum is also one of the flashier of the fixed forms. Its constraints are overt and difficult to conceal. The poem's artifice constantly calls attention to itself. Moreover, its form makes a very specific argument—that trauma is an ouroboros, an endless loop from which the speaker cannot escape.

Incident

We tell the story every year—
how we peered from the windows, shades drawn—
though nothing really happened,
the charred grass now green again.

We peered from the windows, shades drawn,

at the cross trussed like a Christmas tree,
the charred grass still green. Then
we darkened our rooms, lit the hurricane lamps.

At the cross trussed like a Christmas tree,
a few men gathered, white as angels in their gowns.
We darkened our rooms and lit the hurricane lamps,
the wicks trembling in their fonts of oil.

It seemed the angels had gathered, white men in their gowns.
When they were done, they left quietly. No one came.
The wicks trembled all night in their fonts of oil;
by morning the flames had all dimmed.

When they were done, the men left quietly. No one came.
Nothing really happened.
By morning all the flames had dimmed.
We tell the story every year.

Trethewey's "Incident" is a particularly clever handling of the pantoum. "We tell the story every year," the poem begins and ends. The act of retelling is demanded not only by the pantoum's rules but also by the narrative; the speaker's family revisits this memory because they can't help returning to the trauma, its disturbing echoes.

And what is the story? According to the speaker, "nothing really happened." Except we understand that something has happened. The cross burning is a symbolic act that expresses racist hate and that frequently precedes physical violence. It leaves behind a charred shadow. Even once the grass grows back, a recollection of that terror remains embedded in the dirt.

In her juxtaposition of images, Trethewey is also making a pointed argument about the Klansmen in the front yard. The strangers' white robes make them look like "angels." The burned cross on the lawn is "trussed like a Christmas tree." The speaker's memory of this act of intimidation is childlike; she describes the scene (almost) as if it were a holiday postcard. At the same time, the adult speaker draws a historical connection between white supremacy and religious faith. She recognizes that the Klansmen's racism is rooted in slaveholder Christianity.

As with "Incident," James Davis's "An Accident" uses a fixed form to revisit a childhood trauma. His brilliant villanelle recounts a painful memory from the speaker's adolescence when a father slammed the car door on his son's finger. Throughout the poem, the speaker reiterates that this was "an accident" and that he "wasn't in danger." With each repetition, the reader becomes increasingly aware that the violence was deliberate. The father is a danger to the son.

The villanelle, a French form originating during the Renaissance, is comprised of five tercets and a closing quatrain, for a total of nineteen lines. The form utilizes two refrains (labeled *A1* and *A2*) as well as an interlocking rhyme scheme (labeled *a* and *b*). Given the fact that the villanelle's structure is dependent on the repetition of long phrases and that it contains only two rhymes, a villanelle is generally most effective when exploring problems without solutions, obsessions, or actions that are repetitive by nature. Instead of pushing against the tightly wrought music of the poem, it's best to embrace the form's cyclical qualities.

An Accident

The day he slammed the tailgate on my finger,
we'd just unloaded the last of the firewood.
It was an accident. I wasn't in danger.

He said he was sorry, twice. "A real humdinger,"
my father called his handiwork, my hand,
the day he slammed the tailgate on my finger.

I was thirteen, a back-tier church-choir singer.
I'd prayed for a straightening all that I could.
It was an accident. I wasn't in danger

as long as I sang my part. I felt no anger
beyond the usual, mortifying need
the day he slammed the tailgate on my finger.

He shuffled cards. I split the deck. A king or
queen, a flush or straight, I understood
it was an accident. I wasn't in danger.

The nail turned plum, then black, a harbinger
of night, a little sunset in my blood
the day he slammed the tailgate on my finger.
I wasn't an accident. I was a danger.

With a form such as the villanelle, it's important that the refrains evolve or develop new meanings over the length of the poem. Repetition is not mere restatement. The poem's speaker must change; he must come to some kind of realization through the act of reiteration. In "An Accident," the speaker slowly acknowledges his own internalized homophobia. This is a religious household, and the speaker has "prayed for a straightening," doing his best to sing his "part" in the church choir. At the end of the poem, the speaker finally understands what a threat his queerness poses to his father's identity. "I was a danger," he concludes. Davis alters the refrain to reflect this discovery. The insistence that "I wasn't in danger" has been replaced by the realization that his past self—however vulnerable and unsafe—did possess some small power; in his queerness, his inability to be anyone but his true self, the speaker imperils his father's unbending view of the world.

Of course, there are many more fixed forms beyond sonnets, pantoums, and villanelles. I hope you'll consider exploring others, including the ghazal, the sestina, and the triolet, to name a few. I believe that all fixed forms—with their precision and overt displays of craftsmanship—suggest a particular stance toward traumatic experience. These forms argue that, for a moment, we can control the trauma, make it intelligible, even transform the pain into something measured, all while placing the trauma within a larger historical and literary tradition.

Writing Your Way In

1. Write a sonnet (being as strict or loose with the form as you wish). Use the containment of those fourteen lines to name a trauma repeatedly. If you wish to imitate Aaron Smith's approach, repeat a word connected to that trauma in every line of the draft.
2. Write a pantoum (being as strict or loose with the form as you wish). As Trethewey does in "Incident," use the repetitive quality of the pantoum to explore how the mind processes a traumatic memory, going over the past again and again as it searches for a resolution to the pain.
3. Write a villanelle (being as strict or loose with the form as you wish) that recounts a traumatic experience. Use the repetitions of the form to visit and revisit the trauma. What do the refrains allow the speaker to discover about the pain?
4. Invent your own form. Create strict rules or constraints that allow you to express something about trauma that you have not been able to address in free verse. Write at least two poems in this new form.

CHAPTER 20

Hybridities

How does trauma refuse classification?
How does pain blur genre?

In the opening chapter of this book, I analyze Elizabeth Rosner's "The Alphabet of Inadequate Language," an abecedarian that functions as a primer in twentieth-century atrocities. Although Rosner's piece aspires to catalog the horrors of war and genocide, the text itself resists taxonomy. Maybe it should be called a poem. Maybe it is a lyric essay. Maybe it's something in between. In its defiance of categorization, "The Alphabet of Inadequate Language" reveals how trauma too is defiant.

Throughout this book I have tried to offer clearly defined strategies for representing and narrating trauma. But now, in this final chapter, I want to talk about how trauma can lead us toward approaches that reside in ambiguity and haze. In *Bending Genre: Essays on Creative Nonfiction*, Margot Singer and Nicole Walker explain that "we think of genres as fixed and clearly bounded when in fact transgression is the norm." Trauma is also transgressive. It crosses our boundaries. It teaches us that the self is not as fixed as we might have believed. Singer and Walker go on to assert, "Genres are rooted in convention. They are also shape-shifters, in a continual state of flux." Sometimes, when attempting to write of trauma, we turn toward convention. Other times, the appropriate response is to create a poem that is barely recognizable as a poem.

This is hybridity. The poet blends genres because certain pains demand an unclassifiable response. Trauma can leak into many parts of a sufferer's life. Its fluidity requires a destabilizing form.

We associate hybridity with science. For instance, one plant is pollinated with another. The mingling of their seeds produces a hybrid species. But hybridity in literature is seldom the result of a controlled methodology. A piece of writing that's deemed hybrid is given that label because no other name suits it. We call something hybrid after a process of elimination: not a poem, not a short story, not an essay. Therefore, we conclude, this strange text must be an example of hybridity. And the poet who writes a hybrid piece may not begin by engaging intentionally with crossbred forms. Rather, the work teaches the writer that it needs to make an argument about trauma's unruliness and its reluctance to be confined.

Eduardo Galeano's dislocating memoir *The Book of Embraces* unfolds in strange, surreal vignettes to represent the traumas of the exilic condition. Galeano, a Uruguayan journalist, was forced into political exile in 1973 and again in 1976, fleeing first to Argentina and then to Spain.

Exile is fragmentary and episodic, its trauma intermittent, occasionally interrupted by moments of normality. It does not move in a straight line. In *The Book of Embraces*, we are exiled from linear narrative itself. About two thirds of the way through text, Galeano presents three "Dreams at the End of Exile." The expatriate's trauma is depicted as infuriating, ridiculous, and mazelike.

Dreams at the End of Exile / 1

Helena dreamed she was trying to close her suitcase and couldn't, and she pushed down on it with both hands and knelt on it and sat on the top of and stood on the top of it, and it wouldn't budge. Mysteries and belongings gushed from the suitcase that wouldn't close.

Dreams at the End of Exile / 2

Helena was returning to Buenos Aires, but didn't know what language to speak or what currency to use. Standing on the corner of Pueyrredón and Las Heras, she waited for the number 60, which didn't arrive—which would never arrive.

Dreams at the End of Exile / 3

Her glasses were smashed and her keys were missing. She scoured the city for her keys, groping on hands and knees, and when at last she found them, the keys told her that they didn't open any of her doors.

Galeano's three dreams function like parables or fables. They are essayistic in that they attempt to circle around a definition of exile and its accompanying traumas (the word *essay*, after all, comes from the French *essayer*, meaning "to try" or "to endeavor"). They also have the lyric intensity and surrealism of prose poems. Each one begins in medias res—in the middle of the action—so that the reader must hurry to catch up with a story of exile that is already well under way.

In the first of these dreams, the narrator's wife, Helena, attempts to shut a suitcase that refuses to close, "mysteries and belongings" spilling out onto the floor. What does this image symbolize? The exile travels light, but she carries a suitcase with a few precious objects to remember home. If her bag will not shut, then her trip cannot end. Helena must either find a way to seal the suitcase or leave its contents behind. When at last she returns home, she must bring nothing with her. She must arrive empty-handed.

In the second dream, Helena comes to Argentina only to realize she "doesn't know what language to speak or what currency to use." Speech and capital. These are two of the essential ways that an exile creates a temporary home: by exerting some small amount of control through communication and through money. Out-of-step with the vernacular, Helena can't make sense of the currency. She waits forever for a public bus that will never appear.

The third dream makes it clear that once a person has been exiled, these sensations of loss and expulsion continue without end. Helena's glasses are "smashed." Her keys are "missing." She searches throughout Buenos Aires, "groping on her hands and knees," and when she finally locates her keys, she discovers they open nothing. Unable to return home, the exile learns that every city is now blurry and impossible to navigate. All entrances stay locked. Home, both as an idea and as a real location, ceases to exist.

While Galeano's handling of hybridity is surreal, the trauma made funny and weird, a writer like Erika Meitner uses hybrid forms to engage with the nightly news and current events. In "It's Gunna Be All Right," her subject is gun violence in America, as well as the threat of autocracy and the continuing impact of the speaker's ancestral past. It's a vertiginous poem that leaps between the narrative, the lyrical, and the journalistic.

It's Gunna Be All Right

HOW DO YOU SPELL LOVE? asks the Slusser's Chapel Church of God message board out Mount Tabor, where I once worked the polls on election day handing out leaflets of Democratic-party ballots next to a college kid in a Dickies jacket whose family owned a dairy farm the next county over who was doing the same for the Republicans. It was raining that day and everyone who took a leaflet from me was hoping to unelect our Republican congressman, who told me, the one time I was able to speak with him in his office about immigration, that what happened to my family in Auschwitz could only happen in Nazi Germany. That was a few months before Nazis marched through the streets of Charlottesville and Rabbi Tom moved the Torah scrolls from the ark at Congregation Beth Israel for safekeeping in case someone tried to firebomb the building. It is nearly Mother's Day, so the chapel's answer is M-O-M. Farther down the road there's a crow feeding on a roadkill possum, a handbuilt log cabin with a bright red metal roof for sale by owner, a road worker in an orange safety vest flipping his sign from slow to stop at intervals; he waves me through. We are dispossessed and devoured entirely by the space around us. The protest sign my neighbor posts on Facebook says LET'S TAKE A MOMENT TO HONOR THE SACRIFICE OF OUR BRAVE SCHOOL CHILDREN WHO LAY DOWN THEIR LIVES TO PROTECT OUR RIGHT TO BEAR ARMS and on the radio they are talking about Riley Howell, who tackled the gunman at UNC Charlotte last week. "I could see him turning and just thinking he could physically beat the bullets to get to that guy, because I'm sure he didn't really imagine anything else," said his girlfriend's father. When I was handing out leaflets on election day, my son's beloved preschool teacher passed me up, headed to vote toting her baby in a car seat carrier. She was with her husband, who was wearing a shirt with a jacked-up cartoon president on it that read, "Donald Pump Making America Swole Again." When I called after her, when she turned the carrier toward me, I saw that her infant son had casts on both his arms. He had just had surgery on his webbed fingers, she explained, to separate them. Who loves us most? The answer here is always the clouds hovering next to the mountains, out-of-season lights strung around porch rails, tulips burrowing through the earth and opening themselves to the sky. The answer here is always Jesus, but I tell my sons your mother. I tell my sons to run, barricade themselves, hide. I tell my sons not to be a hero or a martyr. Riley Howell was shot three times. The third bullet came as he was inches from the gunman, who fired at point-blank range into his head. A praying mantis is the ultimate mimetic animal, who folds itself into stalklike immobility. Who becomes indistinguishable from the branches on which it sits. Who plays dead to avoid the attention of its predators. Riley Howell's father, Thomas, who works as a trauma nurse, saw his son's body—saw the burn mark along his jawbone that told him the gun muzzle was pressed against his son's skin. As a kid I believed—we all did—that praying mantises were an endangered species and it was illegal to

> kill them, but it turns out this is a long-standing urban myth. It turns out they were never endangered. When my sons were younger, we used to go out at almost sunset to look for praying mantises balanced on boxwood branches in the garden, and then they would run down the hill to the neighbor's trampoline, where they'd propel themselves forward into the humming dusk. The ways in which we fly are bright and numinous. The newspaper recounts Riley Howell's viewing, where his younger cousin Maisie remembered launching herself backward on a trampoline, and almost landing on her head when he reached out. "He caught me in the air," she said, "before I fell."

Meitner demands that the reader keep pace with the poem's rapid movements. The text keeps shifting, and we must follow its gaze as it moves from the local to the global, from the present to the past, and even from the human world to that of insects. Through her handling of form—an expansive prose poem that thinks in the way of a braided essay, intertwining several distinct themes and voices—she argues that all these matters are interconnected. The ongoing trauma of American gun violence is linked to our current impulse toward autocracy, which, in turn, is connected to the speaker's family history in Nazi Germany. One form of bloodshed spills into another. The speaker's advice to her sons, that they "run, barricade themselves, hide" in the case of a school shooting, is given a visual echo in the praying mantis, "who folds itself into stalklike immobility." The poem is breathless and terrified as it trampolines from one idea into the next. Its final gesture is one of falling and of being caught—heroically, by a boy who will be shot when he is only twenty-one—just before disaster.

When we turn to hybridity as a way of considering trauma, we're asserting that extreme emotional and physical pain resists easy ordering. Such wounds, although they're contained within our bodies and our thoughts, maintain their own terrible autonomy. Trauma unsettles. Sometimes it needs a provocative, novel form.

Writing Your Way In

1. Emulate Eduardo Galeano's "Dreams at the End of Exile" and write three linked fables that share the same title. Allow an inanimate object to talk. Focus on the sensory details of the setting. Employ surreal images and lyric language.
2. In the way of Erika Meitner's "It's Gunna Be All Right," write a prose poem that braids together three seemingly different topics. Over the course of the draft, use dialogue, scene-building, and research to show how these traumas are interconnected. Experiment with syntax. Move between ordinary speech and moments of lyricism.

CONCLUSION

After the Post-Traumatic

A few months ago, a friend wrote to me. As she revealed in her message, she was in the middle of a devastating trauma. She couldn't eat. She couldn't sleep. And she couldn't write poems, although she so wanted to document what she was facing, to transcribe her thoughts and feelings in the immediacy of her mid-traumatic moment.

My friend knew I was working on this book. *Is there some strategy,* she asked, *that you can recommend? I need distance,* she said. *But how do I find critical detachment while I'm inside this thing?*

As I read her message, I thought about Erich Auerbach, the noted philologist. Auerbach wrote *Mimesis: The Representation of Reality in Western Literature,* one of the most influential books of literary criticism in the twentieth century, while he was in exile in Turkey, having fled the Nazis. The book isn't about the war or about Auerbach's longing for home. And yet, the first chapter in *Mimesis* contains an exquisite analysis of Book 10 of *The Odyssey*. This is the moment in which Odysseus has finally reached Ithaca, after twenty years in exile. First, he spends ten years fighting in the Trojan Wars. Then, after the conquering of Troy, he spends another decade trying to find his way back to Ithaca, his path halted by twists and turns the interference of the gods.

Auerbach examines the scene in which Odysseus's nursemaid recognizes him, although he's disguised as a drifter dressed in rags. Eurycleia is washing the king's feet in a gesture of Ithacan hospitality. Her wet hand touches a scar on Odysseus's leg, and she knows him. She knows that this destitute man is, in fact, Odysseus. Suddenly, Homer launches into a tremendous flashback. We see in tiny, meticulous detail how Odysseus was stabbed by the tusk of a boar on a hunt many decades ago. We see the torn skin. We see the blood and the violence of the animal killed.

Auerbach's task is to explain the craft of the ancient, epic poet. He's interested in the immediacy of *The Odyssey*; he wants readers to understand that whatever Homer narrates "is for the time being the only present, and fills the both the stage and the reader's mind completely." Auerbach argues that, in contrast to Biblical storytelling where the interiority of characters remains inaccessible and mysterious, Homer allows us to enter it all—places, people, their quietest thoughts—fully: "Clearly outlined, brightly and uniformly illuminated, men and things stand out in a realm where everything is visible; and not less clear—wholly expressible, orderly even in their ardor—are the feelings and thoughts of the persons involved."

Homer's narrative approach is Auerbach's subject. But the wound of trauma—the permanent mark it leaves on us—exists here as well. Maybe Auerbach is even writing about himself, exiled in Istanbul and hoping that, one day, he'll be able return to Germany just as Odysseus does to Ithaca. Maybe he's hoping that the trauma of the current moment will one day become little more than a healed wound by which his loved ones will be able to recognize him.

Czesław Miłosz, a Polish poet who knew something about the traumas of war, genocide, and autocracy, writes in an essay that "people thrown into the middle of events that tear cries of pain from their mouth have difficulty in finding the distance necessary to transform this material artistically."

Which is to say: my friend may not be able to write directly about this agony in which she finds herself. She may need analogy or metaphor to trick herself into writing about the trauma at an acute angle. She may need an Odysseus.

Or maybe, she needs to wait until the hurt has ended.

I have been able to represent trauma in my poetry because I've learned that, while trauma is a wound, ideally the writing of the poem comes *after* the post-traumatic. The poem should be composed once the wound is scabbed over, if not fully healed.

As my friend admitted in her message to me, we need distance. Even when the poem's effect is mimetic—its intention to put readers inside the condition of the traumatized mind—the poet still needs intellectual detachment and some coldness to render such effects. You may find that, before you can use the strategies recommended in this book, you will need therapeutic support to prepare for the writing process. You may even want to seek out the assistance of a trauma-informed writing coach.

Often, when I lecture on this subject, I'm asked about self-care. For me, the work of crafting the poem is the self-care. Because I only write once I am well past the pain, I do not find it distressing to draft poems that engage with trauma. Instead, the unhappiness I experience is that of wrestling with the technical challenges of writing. I am hurt by my own limitations as a writer. My failures bother me—that I so often get the poem wrong.

Near the end of *The Life of Poetry*, Muriel Rukeyser asserts, "For the last time, I wish to say that we will not be saved by poetry. But poetry is the type of creation in which we may live and which will save us." And Gregory Orr writes in *A Primer for Poets and Readers of Poetry*,

> Doesn't everyone, at some time, write a poem or at least want to write one? The expressive impulse can grip us when we're in grief or when we're in joy. Maybe we don't actually write a poem because we don't know how to or don't feel adequate to express what we're experiencing; but we may find solace or release in someone else's poem, as if that person had said it for us. Or maybe we wait a while—maybe we'll live a bit with our confusion before we can

order it. But poetry is there, waiting for us, offering its resources when we're ready to dramatize our experience and shape it into something fixed and stable, yet pulsing with life.

Even when I write a poem that fails, I feel saved by the process of attempting to fasten trauma to the page. Even my faultiest language, to echo Orr, pulses occasionally "with life." For a little while, I live inside that effort to create. Successful or not, the poem is a brief home, and its words shelter me.

Writing any poem is difficult. Sometimes writing poems about pain can seem almost impossible. Much of the first half this book provides techniques for writing poems that represent the experience of being inside the traumatized mind. And many of the later chapters offer rhetorical strategies that poets can use to make arguments about the nature of trauma itself. This book's structure echoes the way that Holocaust historian Dominick LaCapra breaks down the experience of trauma into two categories. The first he calls "acting-out":

> Acting-out is related to repetition, and even the repetition-compulsion—the tendency to repeat something compulsively. This is very clear in the case of people who undergo a trauma. They have a tendency to relive the past, to exist in the present as if they were still fully in the past, with no distance from it. They tend to relive occurrences, or at least find that those occurrences intrude on their present existence, for example, in flashbacks; or in nightmares; or in words that are compulsively repeated, and that don't seem to have their ordinary meaning, because they're taking on different connotations from another situation, in another place.

LaCapra calls the second category "workingthrough":

> In the workingthrough, the person tries to gain critical distance

> on a problem, to be able to distinguish between past, present and future. For the victim, this means his ability to say to himself, "Yes, that happened to me back then. It was distressing, overwhelming, perhaps I can't entirely disengage myself from it, but I'm existing here and now, and this is different from back then."

This is a book both of acting-out and of workingthrough. But whatever your intention—either to immerse readers in the experience of trauma or to offer a more detached, intellectual perspective—the job of writing the poems remains the same. The task is emotional but also cerebral, a critical and clinical engagement with pain. Whether you hope to write poems that act-out or workthrough, you should consider the relationship between form and content. Research your field. Read what's been said already so that you understand how your voice adds to the conversation. Analyze the tropes you employ. Examine your position with respect to the pain.

Confronting trauma can be particularly perilous in a creative writing workshop. Scholar and psychoanalyst Deborah Britzman argues that learning is "a psychic event, charged with resistance to knowledge." She explains that "resistance is a precondition for learning from knowledge and the grounds of knowledge itself. And yet this insight—that difficult knowledge may be refused—is painful to tolerate when the subjects studied are genocide, ethnic hatred, and the experiences of despair and helplessness." Britzman is writing about the pedagogical complexities of teaching painful, traumatic histories such as the Shoah, events that offer what she calls "difficult knowledge." But the concerns she raises are just as pertinent to the workshop. Most creative writing faculty lack the expertise to guide conversations that center on these kinds of wounds. And students often feel unable to offer critiques because they worry the poet is too close to the material and may be damaged, even by the respectful act of close reading. Frequently, in response to their own discomfort, students will minimize the hurt they find in a peer's poem. This can leave the poet frustrated and angry. The poet sees the workshop as a place where art can finally be made from trauma. Instead the work is met with silence, an unwillingness to engage with the text's pain. At times, even empathetic comments from peers—*I'm so sorry this happened to you*—can exasperate the poet, who, having done the necessary therapeutic work, may be eager now for concrete, craft-based feedback. Conversely, if the poet is not yet prepared to write in a rigorous way about trauma, then the text can speak in such coded language that the narrative becomes almost indecipherable. Misinterpretations and misreadings are inevitable then. Few creative writing workshops are up to the task of responding to poems that articulate or enact difficult knowledge.

Therefore, whether you are writing on your own or are part of a workshop, take as much time as the poem needs. Be prepared for how a poem of difficult knowledge may test you in its making and others in its reading. Difficult knowledges challenges both the poet and the audience. Hurt will wait until you are ready to approach it. Then you can search, as Eurycleia once did, compassionately, uncertainly, toward the faded line of a scar.

And after all this, we remain more than our traumas.

When I was writing *The Wounded Line*, there were moments I couldn't remember that much of my own work is concerned with delight: the scent of saffron and roses or, perhaps, my dog, the little assertive sound she makes when it's time to take an afternoon walk and she stamps her gray paws near the closet door where she knows a pink leash hangs from a plastic hook.

I would forget about everything else but grief. Perhaps, in attempting to write poems of trauma, this has also happened to you. Perhaps you have also worried that poems of trauma will become fetishistic or idolatrous, too worshipful of pain. But this needn't be true. Our poems can be evidence of how a speaker survives the worst. Think of the myth of Philomela, a raped girl who is transformed into a nightingale and, in her new form, finds a ceaseless, lyrical voice of lamentation. Think of Brecht, who insists that, in our bleakest hours, "There will be singing / Of the dark times."

During the most difficult moments of drafting this book, I would look up from my computer screen and remember the cup of black tea cooling on the kitchen countertop. There it was—the mug waiting for me, a pale wraith of steam rising from its surface. Already I could imagine the taste of a gingersnap cookie dipped in the dark liquid, the tannin and spice, the sharp crumbs like sand dissolving in sugar on my tongue.

Works Cited

Adorno, Theodor. "Cultural Criticism and Society." *Prisms*. Translated by Shierry Weber Nicholson and Samuel Weber. MIT Press, 1983.

Améry, Jean. *At the Mind's Limits: Contemplations by a Survivor on Auschwitz and Its Realities*. Translated by Sidney Rosenfeld. Indiana University Press, 1980.

Amis, Martin. *Time's Arrow*. Vintage, 1991.

Arendt, Hannah. *Eichmann in Jerusalem: A Report on the Banality of Evil*. Penguin, 1963.

Auerbach, Erich. *Mimesis: The Representation of Reality in Western Literature*. Translated by Willard R. Trasl. Princeton University Press, 2003.

Bachmann, Beth. "Mask." *The New Yorker*, March 30, 2020. https://www.newyorker.com/magazine/2020/04/06/mask.

Balakian, Peter. "Ozone Journal." In *Ozone Journal*. University of Chicago Press, 2015.

Bandura, Valerie. "Breathing Ground." 2024.

Barthes, Roland. *Camera Lucida: Reflections on Photography*. Translated by Richard Howard. Farrar, Strauss and Giroux, 1981.

Beasley, Sandra. "Cherry Tomatoes." In *Theories of Falling*. New Issues Press, 2008.

Brecht, Bertolt. "In the dark times." In *The Collected Poems of Bertolt Brecht*. Translated by David Constantine and Tom Kuhn. Liveright, 2018.

Britzman, Deborah P. *Lost Subjects, Contested Objects: Toward a Psychoanalytic Inquiry of Learning*. State University of New York Press, 1998.

Caruth, Cathy. *Unclaimed Experience: Trauma, Narrative, and History*. Johns Hopkins University Press, 2016.

Celan, Paul. "Deathfugue." *Selected Poems and Prose of Paul Celan*. Translated by John Felstiner. Norton, 2001.

Che, Cathy Linh. "The German word for dream is traume." In *Split*. Alice James Books, 2014.

Choi, Franny. "The World Keeps Ending, and the World Goes On." In *The World Keeps Ending, and the World Goes On*. Ecco, 2023.

Davis, James. "An Accident." *Limp Wrist Magazine*, October 6, 2021. https://www.limpwristmagazine.com/lw4toc.

Derricote, Toi. "Why I don't write about George Floyd." Academy of American Poets, June 23, 2023. https://poets.org/poem/why-i-dont-write-about-george-floyd.

Diagnostic and Statistical Manual of Mental Disorders. 5th ed. American Psychiatric Association, 2013.

Diaz, Natalie. "The Facts of Art." In *When My Brother Was an Aztec*. Copper Canyon Press, 2012.

Dickinson, Emily. "After great pain, a formal feeling comes." In *The Poems of Emily Dickinson*. Edited by R. W. Franklin. Belknap Press, 1998.

Dubrow, Jehanne. "Eros and Psyche." In *The Arranged Marriage*. University of New Mexico Press, 2015.

Espaillat, Rhina P. "Suppose." 2024.

Faizullah, Tarfia. "The Interviewer Acknowledges Shame." In *Seam*. Southern Illinois University Press, 2014.

Farris, Katie. "Tell It Slant." In *Standing in the Forest of Being Alive*. Alice James Books, 2023.

Felman, Shoshana, and Dori Laub. *Testimony: Crises of Witnessing in Literature, Psychoanalysis, and History*. Routledge, 1992.

Forché, Carolyn. *Against Forgetting: Twentieth-Century Poetry of Witness*. Norton, 1993.

Gabbert, Elisa. "Sometimes the Funny Thing About Poetry Is the Poems." *The New York Times*, October 2, 2020. https://www.nytimes.com/2020/10/02/books/review/poetry-chessynormile-great-exodus-great-wall-great-joke-sumita-chakraborty-arrow.html.

Galeano, Eduardo. "Dreams at the End of Exile / 1, 2, and 3." In *The Book of Embraces*. Translated by Cedric Belfrage. Norton, 1992.

Garcia, Daniel. "Reader, I Didn't Leave." *The Lickety-Split*, May 6, 2022. https://x.com/olicketysplit/status/1522632121692549120?s=20&t=tcnk7l6RcEmEmPNNo2_IXQ.

Gay, Ross. *Inciting Joy: Essays*. Algonquin Books, 2022.

Gay, Ross. "A Small Needful Fact." Split This Rock. April 30, 2015. https://www.splitthisrock.org/poetry-database/poem/a-small-needful-fact.

Hall, James Allen. "Inheritance at Corresponding Periods of Life, at Corresponding Seasons of the Year, as Limited by Sex." *The Adroit Journal*, no. 47. https://theadroitjournal.org/issue-forty-seven/james-allen-hall/?amp.

Haslam, Nick, Jesse S. Y. Tse, and Simon de Deyne. "Concept Creep and Psychiatrization." *Frontiers in Sociology*, December 16, 2021. https://www.frontiersin.org/articles/10.3389/fsoc.2021.806147/full.

Hazelton, Rebecca. "Questions About the Wife." In *Vow*. Cleveland State University Poetry Center, 2013.

Herman, Judith. *Trauma and Recovery: The Aftermath of Violence—From Domestic Abuse to Political Terror*. Basic Books, 2022.

Hirsch, Edward. "I was shaking but I was also looking down." In *Gabriel: A Poem*. Knopf, 2014.

Hirsch, Joshua. *Afterimage: Film, Trauma, and the Holocaust*. Temple University Press, 2003.

Hirsch, Marianne. *The Generation of Postmemory: Writing and Visual Culture After the Holocaust*. Columbia University Press, 2012.

"Interviewer Guidelines." USC Shoah Foundation. University of Southern California. 2021. PDF.

Jorgensen, Lucas. "The Bureau of Mercy." *Literary Hub*, May 18, 2023. https://lithub.com/the-bureau-of-mercy/.

Joudah, Fady. "Mimesis." In *Alight*. Copper Canyon Press, 2013.

Kakutani, Michiko. "Books of The Times; Time Runs Backward To Point Up a Moral." *The New York Times*, October 22, 1991. https://archive.nytimes.com/www.nytimes.com/books/98/02/01/home/amis-arrow.html.

Kaminsky, Ilya. "The Poem Is a Warning." Interview by Dan Kois. *Slate*, March 4, 2022. https://slate.com/culture/2022/03/interview-ilya-kaminsky-poet-ukraine.html.

Kaminsky, Ilya. "We Lived Happily During the War." In *Deaf Republic*. Graywolf Press, 2019.

Kolchinsky, Julia. "Featured Poetry: Against Naming By Julia Kolchinsky Dasbach." *New South*, March 7, 2017. https://newsouthjournal.wordpress.com/2017/03/07/featured-poetry-against-naming-by-julia-kolchinsky-dasbach/.

Kolchinsky, Julia. "glossary / глоссарий." *Poetry Magazine*, September 2022, https://www.poetryfoundation.org/poetrymagazine/poems/158388/from-glossary-of-grief.

Kwock Kim, Suji. "Fugue." Academy of American Poets, December 4, 2018, https://poets.org/poem/fugue.

LaCapra, Dominick. *Writing History, Writing Trauma*. Johns Hopkins University Press, 2014.

Lee, Li-Young. "I Ask My Mother to Sing." In *Rose*. BOA Editions, 1986.

Leung, Muriel. "Erasure in Three Acts: An Essay." Poetry Foundation, October 3, 2023. https://www.poetryfoundation.org/harriet-books/2021/11/erasure.

Levin, Phillis. "Introduction." In *The Penguin Book of the Sonnet*. Penguin Books, 2001.

Levine, Peter. *In an Unspoken Voice: How the Body Releases Trauma and Restores Goodness*. North Atlantic Books, 2010.

Lindenberg, Rebecca. "Catalogue of Ephemera." In *Love, an Index*. McSweeney's Publishing, 2012.

Lockwood, Patricia. "Rape Joke." In *Motherland Fatherland Homelandsexuals*. Penguin, 2014.

Long Soldier, Layli. "38." In *WHEREAS*. Graywolf Press, 2017.

Lusby, Lindsay. "Self-Portrait as Psychopomp." 2024.

Meitner, Erika. "It's Gunna Be Alright." *The Southern Review* 56, no. 2 (2020): 280–81.

Miłosz, Czesław. "Ruins and Poetry." In *The Witness of Poetry*. Harvard University Press, 1984.

Morrison, Toni. *Beloved*. Vintage, 1987.

Nethercott, GennaRose. *Thistlefoot*. Anchor Books, 2022.

Orr, Gregory. *Poetry As Survival*. University of Georgia Press, 2002.

Orr, Gregory. *A Primer for Poets and Readers of Poetry*. Norton, 2018.

Ozick, Cynthia. "Rosa." In *The Shawl*. Vintage, 1990.

Pegeen Kelly, Brigit. "Song." In *Song*. BOA Editions, 1995.

Petrosino, Kiki. "What Your Results Mean: Western Africa 28%." In *White Blood: A Lyric of Virginia*. Sarabande Books, 2020.

Raczimow, Henri. "Memory Shot Through with Holes." In *The Holocaust: Theoretical Readings*. Edited by Neil Levi and Michael Rothenberg. Rutgers University Press, 2003.

Rasmussen, Matt. "Reverse Suicide." In *Black Aperture*. Louisiana State University Press, 2013.

Rekdal, Paisley. *Appropriate: A Provocation*. Norton, 2021.

Rosner, Elizabeth. "The Alphabet of Inadequate Language." In *Survivor Café: The Legacy of Trauma and the Labyrinth of Memory*. Counterpoint, 2017.

Rukeyser, Muriel. *The Life of Poetry*. Paris Press, 1996.

Scarry, Elaine. *The Body in Pain: The Making and Unmaking of the World*. Oxford University Press, 1985.

Schneiderman, Jason. "Dramaturgy." In *Self Portrait of Icarus as a Country on Fire*. Red Hen Press, 2024.

Sharif, Solmaz. "The Near Transitive Properties of the Political and Poetical: Erasure." *Evening Will Come: A Monthly Journal of Poetics*, October 3, 2023. https://thevolta.org/ewc28-ssharif-p1.html.

Singer, Margot, and Nicole Walker, eds. *Bending Genre: Essays on Creative Nonfiction*. Bloomsbury, 2013.

Smith, Aaron. "Sissy." Academy of American Poets, March 15, 2023. https://poets.org/poem/sissy.

Smith, Clint. "Counterfactual." In *Counting Descent*. Write Bloody Publishing, 2016.

Smith, Clint. "'We Are Not Singularly Defined by the Things that Kill Us': A Conversation with Clint Smith." GrubWrites, October 23, 2023. grubstreet.org/blog/we-are-not-singularly-defined-by-the-things-that-kill-us-a-conversation-with-clint-smith/.

Smith, Tracy K. "Declaration." In *Wade in the Water*. Graywolf Press, 2018.

Stone, Nomi. "Waiting for Happiness." Academy of American Poets, September 5, 2024, https://poets.org/poem/waiting-happiness.

Theune, Michael. "The Emblem Structure." In *Structure & Surprise: Engaging Poetic Turns*. Edited by Michael Theune. Teachers & Writers Collaborative, 2007.

Torres, Angela Narciso. "Fennel." *32 Poems* 43 (2024): 25.

Tran, Paul. "Landscape with the Fall of Icarus: Oil on Canvas: Pieter Brueghel: 1520." In *All the Flowers Kneeling*. Norton, 2022.

Trethewey, Natasha. "Incident." In *Native Guard*. Houghton Mifflin, 2007.

Turner, Brian. "Phantom Noise." In *Phantom Noise*. Alice James Books, 2010.

Vang, Soul. "Song of the Cluster Bomblet." Academy of American Poets, July 11, 2023. https://poets.org/poem/song-cluster-bomblet.

White, Allison Benis. "Description of Symptoms." Academy of American Poets, March 20, 2023. https://poets.org/poem/description-symptoms.

Yoon, Emily Jungmin. *A Cruelty Special to Our Species*. Harper Collins, 2019.

Yoon, Emily Jungmin. "Inherited Trauma." Interview by Emily Jungmin Yoon. *The Paris Review*, January 16, 2019. https://www.theparisreview.org/blog/2019/01/16/inherited-trauma-an-interview-with-emily-jungmin-yoon/.

Zucker, Rachel. *The Poetry of Wrongness*. Wave Books, 2023.

Permissions

Beth Bachmann, "Mask," copyright © 2020 by Beth Bachmann. Originally published in *The New Yorker* and reprinted with the permission of the author.

Peter Balakian, section 42 of "Ozone Journal," copyright © 2015 by Peter Balakian. Reprinted from *Ozone Journal* with the permission of University of Chicago Press.

Valerie Bandura, "Breathing Ground," copyright © 2024 by Valerie Bandura. Reprinted with the permission of the author.

Sandra Beasley, "Cherry Tomatoes," copyright © 2008 by Sandra Beasley. Reprinted from *Theories of Falling* with the permission of the author.

Bertholt Brecht, "In the dark times" from *The Collected Poems of Bertholt Brecht*, translated by Tom Kuhn and David Constantine. Copyright © 2019, 2015 by Tom Kuhn and David Constantine. Underlying copyright Bertholt-Brecht-Erben / Suhrkamp Verlag. Used by permission of Liveright Publishing Corporation.

Cathy Linh Che, "The German word for dream is trauma," copyright © 2014 by Cathy Linh Che. Reprinted from *Split* with the permission of Alice James Books.

"The World Keeps Ending, and the World Goes On" from *The World*

Keeps Ending, and the World Goes On by Franny Choi. Copyright © 2022 by Franny Choi. Used by permission of HarperCollins Publishers.

James Davis, "An Accident," copyright © 2021 by James Davis. Originally published in *Limp Wrist Magazine* and reprinted with the permission of the author.

Toi Derricote, "Why I don't write about George Floyd," copyright © 2023 by Toi Derricote. Reprinted from the Academy of American Poets website with the permission of the author.

Natalie Diaz, "The Fact of Art," copyright © 2012 by Natalie Diaz. Reprinted from *When My Brother Was an Aztec* with the permission of Copper Canyon Press.

Jehanne Dubrow, "Eros and Psyche," copyright © 2015 by Jehanne Dubrow. Reprinted from *The Arranged Marriage* with the permission of the University of New Mexico Press.

Rhina P. Espaillat, "Suppose," copyright © 2024 by Rhina P. Espaillat. Reprinted with the permission of the author.

Tarfia Faizullah, "The Interviewer Acknowledges Shame," copyright © 2014 by Tarfia Faizullah. Reprinted from *Seam* with the permission of Southern Illinois University Press.

Katie Farris, "Tell It Slant," copyright © 2023 by Katie Farris. Reprinted from *Standing in the Forest of Being Alive* with the permission of Alice James Books.

Eduardo Galeano, "Dreams at the End of Exile / 1, 2, and 3" from *The Book of Embraces*, translated by Cedric Belfrage. Copyright © 1989 by

Eduardo Galeano. English translation copyright © 1991 by Cedric Belfrage. Used by permission of W. W. Norton & Company, Inc.

Daniel Garcia, "Reader, I Didn't Leave," copyright © 2022 by Daniel Garcia. Originally published in *The Lickety-Split* and reprinted with the permission of the author.

"A Small Needful Fact" by Ross Gay was originally published through *Split This Rock*'s The Quarry: A Social Justice Poetry Database (https://www.splitthisrock.org/poetry-database/poem/a-small-needful-fact).

James Allen Hall, "Inheritance at Corresponding Periods of Life, at Corresponding Seasons of the Year, as Limited by Sex," copyright © 2023 by James Allen Hall, Originally published in *The Adroit Journal* and reprinted with the permission of the author.

Rebecca Hazelton, "Questions About the Wife" copyright © 2013 by Rebecca Hazelton. Reprinted from *Vow* with the permission of Cleveland State University Poetry Center.

Lucas Jorgensen, "The Bureau of Mercy," copyright © 2023 by Lucas Jorgensen. Originally published in *Literary Hub* and reprinted with the permission of the author.

Fady Joudah, "Mimesis," copyright © 2013 by Fady Joudah. Reprinted from *Alight* with the permission of Copper Canyon Press.

Ilya Kaminsky, "We Lived Happily During the War," copyright © 2019 by Ilya Kaminsky. Reprinted from *Deaf Republic* with the permission of Graywolf Press.

Suji Kwock Kim, "Fugue," copyright © 2018 by Suji Kwock Kim.

Reprinted from Academy of American Poets website with the permission of the author.

Julia Kolchinsky, "glossary / глоссарий," copyright © 2022 by Julia Kolchinsky. Originally published in *Poetry Magazine* and reprinted with the permission of the author.

Rebecca Lindenberg, "Catalogue of Ephemera," copyright © 2012 by Rebecca Lindenberg. Reprinted from *Love, an Index* with the permission of McSweeney's Publishing. Originally published by McSweeney's.

Lindsay Lusby, "Self-Portrait as Psychopomp," copyright © 2024 by Lindsay Lusby. Reprinted with the permission of the author.

Erika Meitner, "It's Gunna Be Alright," copyright © 2020 by Erika Meitner. Originally published in *The Southern Review* and reprinted with the permission of the author.

Brigit Pegeen Kelly, "Song," copyright © 1995 by Brigit Pegeen Kelly. Reprinted from *Song* with the permission of BOA Editions.

Matt Rasmussen, "Reverse Suicide," copyright © 2013 by Matt Rasmussen. Reprinted from *Black Aperture* with the permission of Louisiana State University Press.

Elizabeth Rosner, "The Alphabet of Inadequate Language," copyright © 2017 by Elizabeth Rosner. Reprinted from *Survivor Café: The Legacy of Trauma and the Labyrinth of Memory* with the permission of Counterpoint Press.

Jason Schneiderman. "Dramaturgy," copyright © 2024 by Jason Schneiderman. Reprinted from *Self Portrait of Icarus as a Country on Fire* with the permission of Red Hen Press.

Aaron Smith, "Sissy," copyright © 2023 by Aaron Smith. Reprinted from Academy of American Poets website with the permission of the author.

Clint Smith, "Counterfactual," copyright © 2016 by Clint Smith. Reprinted from *Counting Descent* with the permission of Write Bloody Publishing.

Tracy K. Smith, "Declaration," copyright © 2018 by Tracy K. Smith. Reprinted from *Wade in the Water* with the permission of Graywolf Press.

Nomi Stone, "Waiting for Happiness," copyright © 2024 by Nomi Stone. Reprinted from the Academy of American Poets website with the permission of the author.

Angela Narciso Torres, "Fennel," copyright © 2024 by Angela Narciso Torres. Originally published in *32 Poems* and reprinted with the permission of the author.

Brian Turner, "Phantom Noise," copyright © 2010 by Brian Turner. Reprinted from *Phantom Noise* with the permission of Alice James Books.

Soul Vang, "Song of the Cluster Bomblet," copyright © 2023 by Soul Vang. Reprinted from the Academy of American Poets website with the permission of the author.

Allison Benis White, "Description of Symptoms," copyright © 2023 by Allison Benis White. Reprinted from the Academy of American Poets website with the permission of the author.

Index